Classics

GLOUCESTERSHIRE
COUNTY CRICKET CLUB

BANQUET

HELD ON

MONDAY, JUNE 24TH, 1895, at the VICTORIA ROOMS, CLIFTON,

TO

MR W. G. GRACE

in Celebration of his

ONE HUNDREDTH "CENTURY,"

Completed on GLOUCESTERSHIRE COUNTY GROUND in match

SOMERSETSHIRE v GLOUCESTERSHIRE,

on FRIDAY MAY 17TH 1895.

HIS GRACE THE DUKE OF BEAUFORT, K.G.,

President

Classics

GLOUCESTERSHIRE
COUNTY CRICKET CLUB

ANDREW HIGNELL

TEMPUS

Frontispiece: A major landmark in W.G. Grace's career.

First published 2004

Tempus Publishing Limited
The Mill, Brimscombe Port,
Stroud, Gloucestershire, GL5 2QG
www.tempus-publishing.com

© Andrew Hignell, 2004

British Library Cataloguing in Publication Data.
A catalogue record for this book is available from the British Library.

ISBN 0 7524 3212 5

Typesetting and origination by Tempus Publishing Limited
Printed and bound in Great Britain

Preface

Nobody could ever claim to compile a definitive list of the fifty best matches played by a county side. Therefore, this is a collection of fifty of some of the finest first-class matches played by Gloucestershire CCC during their illustrious history – years that have seen some of the greatest names in cricket history play with distinction for the West Country side.

In compiling this collection of classic matches, I have tried not to let either emotion or personal choice affect the final choice. Having not seen games before 1970, I have relied on the crystal-clear memories and astute views of other writers and observers of West Country cricket. By talking to Keith Gerrish, the late Bert Avery, Keith Ball and the late Grahame Parker, as well as reading the wonderful prose of Alan Gibson and David Foot, I feel I have successfully maintained an objectivity in terms of what was collectively best for Gloucestershire CCC.

Inevitably, there are omissions – none though that I feel are too major in terms of the wider picture and the history of Gloucestershire. With this in mind, I have ignored Wally Hammond's final game for the county as well as some of the personal milestones such as W.G. Grace reaching 1,000 runs in for the first time in May 1885, Tony Brown taking seven catches in an innings at Trent Bridge in 1966, and the match in 1953 against Hampshire when Andy Wilson, that fine wicketkeeper, pouched ten catches in the game. Fine feats they may all have been, and achievements that remain as county records, but this is a book that largely focuses on thrilling encounters and collective feats in the first-class game.

My thanks to Keith Gerrish, the county's scorer and statistician for the detailed scorecards, and checking the text. Thanks also to Paul McGregor, Stephen Chalke, Chris Brain, Ken Faulkner, David Smith and Peter Perchard for assistance with the images, as well as to photographers Hugh John, Adrian Murrell, David Munden, George Herringshaw and Bill Smith for some of the wonderful images. Other photographs and memorabilia come from the county's archives, or from my own private collection. Thanks are also due to David Green for penning the foreword, and recalling the events of a wonderful match against Sussex in 1968 – the fifty-first classic match in this book – and also to my wife Debra for her support as my mind turned again to another cricket book.

Andrew Hignell
St. Fagan's, Cardiff
September 2004

Foreword

By David Green

My association with Gloucestershire began in 1968 when I joined them as a player after Lancashire – a county I had followed since I was a boy of nine and for whom I had played between 1959 and 1967 – had not renewed my contract at the end of the 1967 season.

Lancashire had good reason for their decision, for after a season and a half of poor form, compounded at times by injury, my batting technique was shot to pieces and my confidence very low. Nevertheless, Gloucestershire officials treated me as a valuable commodity; virtually all the players were welcoming and Arthur Milton and John Mortimore in particular set to work to rebuild my batting, largely from scratch.

After a miserable start to the campaign, during which my top score from sixteen innings was 34 and my average 14, I began to play rather well, so much so that I was first in the country to 2,000 runs. The only others to reach the mark that year were Richards, B.A., and Edrich, J.H. – not bad company for a hacker! After such a change in fortunes, it is small wonder that I remain to this day devoted to Gloucestershire's cause.

At the end of July 1968, we had a remarkable game with Sussex at Hove. That year a number of Championship matches, as an experiment, included Sunday play and our preceding contest with Leicestershire, which we lost by four wickets was one of these. We therefore travelled down to Hove on the Tuesday and with all day to do it in, our party, consisting of Milton, the captain that year, Mike Procter, also in his first season with the club, and myself did not hurry too much.

We dawdled through the Midlands, hitting London with the rush hour in full swing. Emerging south of the Thames, all three of us hot and thirsty, we stopped for a beer and later, as one did in those pre-breathalyser days, we stopped for one or two more.

The upshot was that when we eventually reached the Imperial Hotel in Hove, it was around 11.30 p.m., and the bar was closed. This seemed a great tragedy to us, but a resourceful night porter saved the day, producing a bottle of Scotch for Milton to have a sip of, and, since Procter's and my preferred beverage at the time was Black & Tan, a crate of bottled Guinness and a crate of light ale. We had made significant inroads into these provisions when someone spotted that it was getting light, so we went to bed.

From left to right: David Green, Mike Procter and Arthur Milton.

We got to the ground at around 10.30 a.m., an hour before the start, with Milton and I, who were to open the innings, both feeling pretty seedy and naturally keen to avoid batting. Procter similarly was not keen to come rushing in off his normal thirty-yard run until his head felt a bit better. The pitch looked a bit green, and the pavilion boundary was little more than fifty yards, both good reasons, as Milton and I agreed, for choosing to bat last.

Procter was panicking as the coin went up, but jubilant when Sussex skipper Mike Griffith put us in after Milton had called incorrectly. Griffith, who had just taken over the captaincy following the mid-season resignation of Jim Parks, was a Cambridge Blue and the son of the current secretary of the MCC, Billy Griffith, who had represented Sussex, Cambridge University and England as a wicketkeeper-batsman. Procter immediately went to sleep in the dressing room while Arthur and I, in some foreboding, put on our pads.

Astonishingly, things went well for us as, stopping the straight ones and nurdling one or two off the others, we reached lunch at 120 for none, both sweating buckets in the hot sun. During the second session, by now feeling remarkably fit, we added exactly 190 runs and had moved onto 315 – then a Championship record opening stand for the county – when Arthur departed just after tea for a chanceless 122. We thrashed on, Procter finally waking up and making a violent 49, and reached 485 for 6 by the close, with my share being a career-best 233.

'Proc', suffering from the damaged thigh that soon afterwards ended his season, could bowl only 7 overs, but Tony Brown, David Smith and John Mortimore fiddled them out for 252, which would have been a lot less without Tony Greig's fine 117. In their second innings, Sussex batted very consistently to make 361, which left us 24 overs to chase 129 – no doddle even on so good a pitch, particularly after we had spent the best part of two days in the field. An excellent contest ended happily for us as we scrambled home with four wickets and nine balls remaining.

On that first evening, Mike Griffith, his insertion having so completely backfired, was looking a little glum in the home dressing room. Then their senior pro, Ken Suttle said to him 'Never mind, Michael, I remember a Sussex captain putting the opposition in, and they made over 500.' Mike cheered up a bit at this. 'Oh, who was that?' he asked. 'It was your effing Dad!' replied Suttle.

SUSSEX v GLOUCESTERSHIRE

Played at Hove on 24th, 25th, 26th July 1968 — Toss: Sussex
Gloucestershire beat Sussex by 4 wickets

GLOUCESTERSHIRE

Batsman			1st				2nd
D.M.Green	c Griffith	b A.Buss	233			b Greig	48
C.A.Milton *	lbw	b A.Buss	122				
R.B.Nicholls		b Jones	0	(2) c Suttle		b Jones	15
D.R.Shepherd	c Greig	b Jones	25	(3) c Greig		b Jones	9
M.J.Procter	c Lenham	b A.Buss	49	(4)		b Greig	11
A.S.Brown	lbw	b Greig	3	(5)		b Greig	8
M.Bissex	not	out	18	(6)	not	out	18
J.B.Mortimore	not	out	18	(7)	run	out	18
B.J.Meyer +				(8)	not	out	0
D.R.Smith							
J.Davey							
Extras	(b 3, lb 13, w 1)		17	(lb 2)			2
TOTAL	(for 6 wkts dec)		485	(for 6 wkts)			129

SUSSEX

Batsman			1st				2nd
L.J.Lenham		b Procter	6	c Bissex		b Mortimore	86
T.B.Racionzer	c Meyer	b Smith	36	c	sub	b Mortimore	82
K.G.Suttle	c Green	b Smith	14			b Brown	5
A.W.Greig	c Meyer	b Brown	117	c Bissex		b Mortimore	4
J.M.Parks +	c Milton	b Mortimore	17	c Bissex		b Brown	49
M.G.Griffith *	c Brown	b Mortimore	4			b Brown	42
M.A.Buss		b Mortimore	22	(8) c Bissex		b Davey	13
G.C.Cooper	c Meyer	b Davey	2	(7)		c & b Bissex	45
E.J.Lewis		b Brown	5	c Bissex		b Davey	6
A.Buss	not	out	19		not	out	11
A.A.Jones	c Meyer	b Smith	4	c Meyer		b Bissex	14
Extras	(lb 5, w 1)		6	(lb 13, nb 1)			14
TOTAL			252				361

SUSSEX	O	M	R	W	O	M	R	W
A.Buss	28	7	77	3	11	0	55	0
Jones	23	1	102	2	6	0	45	2
M.A.Buss	14	2	53	0				
Greig	27	1	130	1	5.3	1	27	3
Lewis	16	1	59	0				
Suttle	12	1	47	0				

GLOUCESTERSHIRE	O	M	R	W	O	M	R	W
Procter	7	0	20	1				
Davey	17	1	61	1	29	2	108	2
Brown	11	3	39	2	30	7	92	3
Smith	15.5	4	63	3	16	5	45	0
Mortimore	21	5	63	3	35	10	81	3
Bissex					7	3	15	2
Green					2	0	6	0

FALL OF WICKETS

	G	S	S	G
	1st	1st	2nd	2nd
1st	315	10	167	34
2nd	316	55	176	55
3rd	374	64	186	74
4th	398	107	187	89
5th	401	119	256	98
6th	453	175	295	126
7th		190	319	
8th		212	327	
9th		235	351	
10th		252	361	

Umpires: C.S.Elliott and A.Jepson

Gloucestershire CCC Classic Matches

1872	v. Yorkshire at Sheffield	10
1876	v. Yorkshire at Cheltenham	12
1877	v. Nottinghamshire at Cheltenham	16
1893	v. Somerset at Cheltenham	18
1903	v. Sussex at Hove	21
1904	v. Somerset at Bristol	24
1906	v. Essex at Bristol	28
1907	v. Northamptonshire at Gloucester Spa	30
1909	v. Middlesex at Bristol	32
1920	v. Somerset at Bristol	34
1922	v. Yorkshire at Bristol	38
1924	v. Middlesex at Bristol	40
1925	v. Essex at Gloucester	44
1925	v. Lancashire at Old Trafford	46
1928	v. Surrey at Cheltenham	48
1928	v. Worcestershire at Cheltenham	50
1930	v. Australians at Bristol	52
1933	v. West Indians at Bristol	56
1935	v. South Africans at Cheltenham	58
1936	v. Indians at Cheltenham	60
1936	v. Nottinghamshire at Gloucester	62
1937	v. Worcestershire at Cheltenham	64
1938	v. Lancashire at Bristol	66

1939	*v.* Kent at Bristol	68
1947	*v.* Yorkshire at Bristol	70
1947	*v.* Middlesex at Cheltenham	72
1948	*v.* Australians at Bristol	76
1949	*v.* Derbyshire at Chesterfield	78
1956	*v.* Somerset at Taunton	80
1957	*v.* Warwickshire at Edgbaston	82
1959	*v.* Essex at Leyton	84
1959	*v.* Surrey at Gloucester	86
1960	*v.* South Africans at Bristol	88
1966	*v.* Warwickshire at Edgbaston	90
1972	*v.* Essex at Westcliff-on-Sea	92
1976	*v.* Somerset at Taunton	96
1977	*v.* Worcestershire at Cheltenham	98
1977	*v.* Sussex at Cheltenham	100
1979	*v.* Indians at Bristol	102
1979	*v.* Leicestershire at Bristol	104
1985	*v.* Derbyshire at Derby	106
1985	*v.* Warwickshire at Cheltenham	108
1986	*v.* Sussex at Bristol	110
1987	*v.* Derbyshire at Bristol	112
1988	*v.* Surrey at Cheltenham	114
1992	*v.* Sussex at Cheltenham	116
1995	*v.* Glamorgan at Abergavenny	118
1996	*v.* Northamptonshire at Bristol	122
1997	*v.* Derbyshire at Cheltenham	124
1998	*v.* Essex at Colchester	126

YORKSHIRE

The name W.G. Grace is synonymous with some of the greatest achievements in Gloucestershire's history and his remarkable achievements take centre stage in the early days of the club, which largely through the efforts of the Doctor (right) and his brothers, became one of the strongest and most revered in England. More than a hundred years have elapsed since the immortal Doctor played his final match for Gloucestershire, yet many of his prodigious feats with both bat and ball remain as club records, and several are unlikely to ever be surpassed.

An example of his outstanding all-round abilities came in July 1872 when Gloucestershire met Yorkshire at the Bramall Lane ground in Sheffield – a fixture which contemporaries regarded as a north-south battle between some of the country's finest cricketers and a joust for supremacy in the embryonic County Championship.

This game had also been chosen by Roger Iddison, Yorkshire's long-serving professional, as his benefit match and the mouth-watering prospect of seeing so many talented cricketers, as well as watching W.G. bat at Bramall Lane for the first time, drew a crowd in excess of 17,000. Even though morning rain delayed the start on the first day, the spectators were not to be disappointed as W.G. and Tom Matthews added 208 without loss before another storm ended play shortly after five o'clock.

The Doctor's share on the opening day was 132* as he treated all of the highly experienced Yorkshire bowlers with complete disdain, twice hitting the ball out of the ground, and scoring 12 in one over from Luke Greenwood. W.G. added a further 18 on the second day before Luke Greenwood gained revenge with the help of brother Andrew who held onto a catch from Grace. But W.G. was not content to rest on his laurels, and when Yorkshire started batting at 4.30 p.m., he opened the bowling with his brother E.M. By the close, the two Graces bowled out the northern county for just 66, with W.G. taking 8/33.

Yorkshire followed on the next day, but they faired only slightly better as W.G. bowled unchanged from one end, with E.M., Fred, and the off-spin of Robert Miles at the other. W.G. added a further seven victims to his match haul as his team wrapped up a comprehensive innings victory, much to the chagrin of the Tykes. Several had really fancied their chances bowling to the Doctor on their own wicket at Bramall Lane. Tom Emmett was disconsolate afterwards saying 'He dab 'em, but seldom, and when he do dab 'em, he dabs 'em for four. I think he should be made to play with a littler bat!'

As was the custom, Gloucestershire batted again before the close in order to entertain the sizeable crowd, many of whom were eager to see the Doctor bat again. But there was to be no encore, as W.G. was caught at midwicket by Lumb for 2. It should not be forgotten that at the time, apart from hits out of the ground, everything had to be run, so apart from his two sixes, the fifteen-stone bewhiskered giant had run 138 of his 150 runs. When added to his 60.1 overs, bowling

```
                         YORKSHIRE v GLOUCESTERSHIRE

Played at Sheffield on 29th, 30th, 31st July 1872          Toss: Gloucestershire
Gloucestershire beat Yorkshire by an innings and 112 runs

                              GLOUCESTERSHIRE
W.G.Grace *        c A.Greenwood b L.Greenwood 150
T.G.Matthews       c Pinder      b Freeman      85
E.M.Grace          st Pinder     b Freeman      11
F.Townsend                       b Freeman       3
G.F.Grace                        b Freeman       3
G.Strachan                       b L.Greenwood  12
F.R.Price +            not           out        10
F.A.Carter             run           out         3
R.F.Miles          c Clayton     b L.Greenwood   3
H.S.Cobden                       b Freeman       4
J.A.Bush             absent         ill
     Extras        (b 2, lb 8)                  10
                                               ---
     TOTAL                                     294

                                 YORKSHIRE
E.B.Rawlinson    c Miles      b W.G.Grace  19 ( 7)       run          out     47
A.Hill           c E.M.Grace  b W.G.Grace   3 ( 9)              b W.G.Grace    1
A.Greenwood      c Townsend   b W.G.Grace   0 ( 5) c G.F.Grace  b W.G.Grace    0
E.Lockwood                    b W.G.Grace   6 ( 3) c G.F.Grace  b W.G.Grace   15
G.Freeman        st Price     b W.G.Grace   1 ( 2) c Strachan   b W.G.Grace    0
J.Rowbotham *    c G.F.Grace  b W.G.Grace  14       c Price      b W.G.Grace   10
R.Iddison              c & b W.G.Grace       4 ( 4) st Price     b Miles       34
E.Lumb           c E.M.Grace  b W.G.Grace   0       c E.M.Grace  b Miles        0
L.Greenwood      c W.G.Grace  b E.M.Grace  12 ( 1) c E.M.Grace  b W.G.Grace    0
G.Pinder +                    b E.M.Grace   0       c Carter     b W.G.Grace    0
R.O.Clayton          not          out        0         not          out        0
     Extras      (b 1, lb 1, w 5)            7       (b 7, lb 1, w 1)           9
                                           ---                                ---
     TOTAL                                  66                                116

YORKSHIRE         O    M    R   W       O    M    R    W      FALL OF WICKETS
Freeman         72.3  32   97   5                            G    Y    Y
L.Greenwood       52  21   83   3                           1st  1st  2nd
Lockwood          10   1   31   0                     1st  238   24    0
Hill              18   5   45   0                     2nd  244   24    3
Clayton            7   3   19   0                     3rd  251   30   25
Iddison            2   0    9   0                     4th  255   32   25
                                                     5th  272   33   35
GLOUCESTERSHIRE                                      6th  277   52  113
W.G.Grace         24  12   33   8    36.1  17   46   7      7th  284   52  113
E.M.Grace         23   9   26   2      5    3    5   0      8th  289   66  116
G.F.Grace                             17    2   35   0      9th  294   66  116
Miles                                 14    5   21   2     10th       66  116

Umpires: C.K.Pullin and F.R.Reynolds
```

unchanged throughout the match, this represented a massive workload, yet the Doctor rarely showed any signs of fatigue.

His achievements are even more remarkable considering the many hours he spent travelling by train, sometimes from one end of the country to the other, and all at a time when railway accidents were commonplace. Yet the Doctor was immune to these perils and the discomfort of long journeys, and he proceeded week-in, week-out to record some of the finest performances with bat and ball in the history of Gloucestershire CCC.

YORKSHIRE

17, 18, 19 August 1876 at Cheltenham

'I do not think I ever played on a better wicket than the one which had been prepared (in 1876) at Cheltenham.' So wrote W.G. in his memoirs recalling the match against Yorkshire that saw the immortal Doctor record the highest ever individual score in Gloucestershire's history and continue a remarkable run of record setting in what became an *annus mirabilis* for the great cricketer.

1876 was certainly the year of Grace, as W.G. amassed 2,622 runs. This fixture against Yorkshire came during a real purple patch in mid-August, and only a few days after the master batsman had recorded the inaugural triple hundred in first-class cricket by scoring 344 for the MCC against Kent. He followed this up with 177 in the space of three hours against Nottinghamshire at Clifton, and just for good measure, he took 8/69 in the second innings as the visitors were humbled by ten wickets.

As they were waiting for a connection on their homeward journey at Cheltenham Spa, the defeated Nottinghamshire team met up with the Yorkshire team heading to Cheltenham and some

The Doctor going out to bat.

A square-cut by the immortal W.G.

of the Trent Bridge professionals ribbed the Tykes about what lay in store, and what prodigious feats the Doctor would produce next. Tom Emmett, the hard-bitten Yorkshire professional, laughed off the mickey-taking, saying 'the big 'un has exhausted himself and cannot do the century trick thrice in succession. Anyhow, if he does I mean to shoot him in the interests of the game, and I know there will be general rejoicing among the professionals at least!'

There were few smiles on the Yorkshire faces as W.G. won the toss and then roasted the Yorkshire attack to score the first ever triple hundred in the County Championship. He made his intensions plain to the Yorkshire attack as he strode out the wicket, saying 'You'll have to get me out today. I shan't get myself out!' He was true to his word and by the end of the day, he had 216 runs to his name. The story goes that some of the Yorkshire professionals refused to bowl at Grace, while another was so scared that he deliberately delivered three of the widest wides ever seen so that he could be taken off.

There was rain on the second morning, but thousands of spectators turned up in anticipation of seeing the Doctor score another 300. With more than a passing glance at the club's coffers, W.G.

YORKSHIRE

E.M. Grace

chivvied the umpires and the Yorkshire team back onto the field and play resumed in the early afternoon. Wickets fell as the Doctor approached 300 and when the ninth wicket fell with the score on 466, it looked as if W.G. might be deprived of the record. But in strode 'Frizzie' Bush, the county's number eleven and wicketkeeper, and a close friend of the Doctor's. Bush had been best man at the Doctor's wedding so he told his great pal 'Don't worry. I'll stay with you until you get your runs.'

'Frizzie' was true to his word, as he stoutly defended, as well as despatching into the outfield some of the more wayward deliveries from the Yorkshire bowlers who had now become quite tired in the face of Grace's wonderful innings. The Doctor duly reached the historic landmark of 300, and when Bush was finally bowled by George Ulyett, W.G. was unbeaten on 318. He departed the College ground to tumultuous applause, and took his aggregate in his past three innings to an astonishing 839 runs at an average of 419.50.

GLOUCESTERSHIRE v YORKSHIRE

Played at Cheltenham College on 17th, 18th, 19th August 1876   Toss: Gloucestershire
Match Drawn

GLOUCESTERSHIRE

W.G.Grace *	not	out	318
E.M.Grace	c sub	b Armitage	5
W.R.Gilbert		b Armitage	40
F.Townsend	st Pinder	b Armitage	0
G.F.Grace		b Emmett	0
W.O.Moberly	c Myers	b Emmett	103
R.E.Bush	c Lister	b Clayton	0
C.R.Filgate		b Clayton	1
E.J.Taylor	run	out	1
R.F.Miles		b Clayton	4
J.A.Bush +		b Ulyett	32
Extras	(b 12, lb 8, w 4)		24

TOTAL			528

YORKSHIRE

E.Lockwood *	hit wicket	b W.G.Grace	23
M.Myers	not	out	46
B.Lister	c J.A.Bush	b Miles	1
D.Eastwood	c W.G.Grace	b Miles	4
T.Emmett		b Gilbert	39
G.Ulyett	c Filgate	b W.G.Grace	4
T.Armitage	c G.F.Grace	b Gilbert	1
A.Hill	run	out	6
R.O.Clayton			
G.Pinder +			
-			
Extras	(w 3)		3

TOTAL	(for 7 wkts)		127

YORKSHIRE	O	M	R	W
Hill	16	2	64	0
Armitage	31	3	100	3
Emmett	51	18	94	2
Lockwood	14	2	35	0
Myers	4	2	4	0
Eastwood	12	4	21	0
Ulyett	25	7	64	1
Clayton	57	18	122	3

GLOUCESTERSHIRE				
G.F.Grace	17	7	34	0
W.G.Grace	36	17	48	2
Miles	15	8	23	2
Townsend	8	0	10	0
Gilbert	8	5	9	2

FALL OF WICKETS

	G	Y
	1st	1st
1st	9	39
2nd	166	40
3rd	167	44
4th	168	110
5th	429	119
6th	430	120
7th	446	127
8th	449	
9th	466	
10th	528	

Umpires: C.K.Pullin and J.Rowbotham

NOTTINGHAMSHIRE

13, 14, 15 August 1877 at Cheltenham

W.G. was also a very skilful and crafty bowler, initially as a round-arm quickie, before switching to slow-medium pace and relying on flight and guile rather than sheer pace. This classic match in 1877 saw Grace in his quicker style, and the Doctor returned both career-best figures in Nottinghamshire's first innings as well as match figures that stood for almost fifty years as the best in Gloucestershire's history.

The game began with Gloucestershire making 235 in their first innings, with run-scoring being quite difficult early on. W.G. took an uncharacteristic forty minutes to score 6 runs, but the innings was subsequently given an impetus by Fred Grace, the youngest of the Grace brothers, who hit 83 and shared an invaluable stand with his elder brother, Edward Mills Grace, as Gloucestershire reached their useful total.

The visitors must have been rueing the sight of W.G. as he proceeded to open the bowling with Billy Midwinter, the Australian international, who was the first professional to play for Gloucestershire. W.G. was soon among the wickets as he scythed his way through the visitors' batting, fully exploiting the damp conditions, and their rather indeterminate strokes, to return figures of 9/55, as the visitors were forced to follow-on.

Despite his first-innings exertions, W.G. continued as Nottinghamshire began their second innings, and together with his brother Fred, he soon polished off the visitors' resistance. W.G. had positioned Fred and Walter Gilbert in his leg-trap, and maintaining a line on leg stump he was delighted to see a series of Nottinghamshire batsmen fall into his trap.

Richard Daft, the visiting captain, had become increasingly irate by the seemingly gullible way his men had given their wickets away to Grace in the first innings, but second time around he was the first to fall into the trap, as Gilbert held onto an easy catch. Grace had overheard Daft's

W.G. Grace, from the front cover of *Man of the World* magazine in August 1880.

```
                    GLOUCESTERSHIRE v NOTTINGHAMSHIRE

Played at Cheltenham College on 13th, 14th, 15th August 1877    Toss: Gloucestershire
Gloucestershire beat Nottinghamshire by an innings and 45 runs

                              GLOUCESTERSHIRE
W.G.Grace *        c Selby      b Morley      17
W.R.Gilbert        c Sherwin    b Barnes      19
W.E.Midwinter                   b Miles       19
G.F.Grace          c Selby      b Daft        83
F.Townsend                      b Morley      10
E.M.Grace          c Wyld       b Morley      43
W.O.Moberly +                   b Morley       5
W.Fairbanks        c Sherwin    b Morley       1
J.Cranston                      b Barnes      23
E.J.Taylor         c Oscroft    b Daft         0
F.G.Monkland          not          out         6
    Extras         (b 5, lb 1, w 3)            9
                                             ---
    TOTAL                                     235

                              NOTTINGHAMSHIRE
R.Daft *       c G.F.Grace  b W.G.Grace    7  ( 5) c Gilbert   b W.G.Grace   0
W.Oscroft                   b Midwinter    9  ( 1) c G.F.Grace b W.G.Grace   7
A.Shrewsbury          c & b W.G.Grace     35        run        out          32
R.Tolley                    b W.G.Grace   11  ( 6) c Gilbert   b W.G.Grace   3
P.W.H.Miles                 b W.G.Grace    5  ( 7)             b W.G.Grace   0
F.Wyld         c E.M.Grace  b W.G.Grace    0  ( 4) c Gilbert   b W.G.Grace   2
J.Selby        c Cranston   b W.G.Grace   19  ( 2)             b Gilbert    30
W.Barnes       c E.M.Grace  b W.G.Grace    8  ( 9)             lbw b W.G.Grace  0
J.Tye                       b W.G.Grace    9  ( 8) c Gilbert   b W.G.Grace   5
F.Morley            not        out         2        c Taylor   b W.G.Grace   0
M.Sherwin +                 b W.G.Grace    5        not        out           0
    Extras         (b 1)                    1
                                          ---                               ---
    TOTAL                                  111                               79
```

NOTTINGHAMSHIRE	O	M	R	W	O	M	R	W	FALL OF WICKETS			
										G	N	N
Morley	83	57	63	5						1st	1st	2nd
Barnes	45.1	22	50	2					1st	29	12	14
Tye	20	10	28	0					2nd	37	17	69
Miles	9	5	11	1					3rd	95	30	70
Tolley	4	0	25	0					4th	125	40	71
Selby	11	4	12	0					5th	195	40	74
Daft	15	2	37	2					6th	205	86	74
									7th	210	88	74
GLOUCESTERSHIRE									8th	225	104	74
W.G.Grace	51	23	55	9	25.1	13	34	8	9th	225	105	74
Midwinter	42	26	37	1	19	12	24	0	10th	235	111	79
Townsend	8	1	18	0								
Gilbert					9	5	12	1				
E.M.Grace					3	1	9	0				

```
Umpires: C.K.Pullin and R.Carpenter
```

remonstrations to his colleagues, so he let out a huge roar of laughter as Gilbert pouched the ball, and Daft departed with a face like thunder!

Arthur Shrewsbury briefly offered some resistance, but on the final morning after heavy rain had fallen, batting became nigh on impossible. On 32, Shrewsbury was stumped by William Moberley, the Clifton schoolmaster and English rugby international, before W.G. finished off the innings with 8/34. The last seven wickets had fallen without a run being scored in the space of twenty-five balls, and to loud applause, W.G. walked off with match figures of 17/89.

SOMERSET

14, 15, 16 August 1893 at Cheltenham

The austere portals of Cheltenham College have witnessed many classic encounters, especially when the eagerly awaited festival has included matches against the touring team or local derbies with Somerset or Worcestershire. In the case of 1893, the annual festival had both, with a match against the touring Australians, plus a contest against Somerset.

For once, Somerset were relishing the opportunity to play their West Country neighbours, as Gloucestershire were without W.G., who was on duty at The Oval for England against Australia. Their pre-match optimism proved well founded as Somerset ended up winning the match by 127 runs, but not before a remarkable and unsurpassed feat involving Charles Townsend, who was one of several colts in the Gloucestershire side, besides being the godson of W.G.

The previous match against Middlesex at Bristol had witnessed the county debuts of both Townsend, the sixteen-year-old leg-spinner, plus W.G. Grace junior, the nineteen-year-old son of the famous Doctor as the county introduced some new faces in a bid to unearth some fresh talent and inject a bit of life into what had become rather a drab season.

Despite conceding 151 runs in 70 overs at Bristol, Townsend retained his place in the side for the match at Cheltenham, and the fresh-faced youngster must have travelled up to the Cotswold town with more than a hint of trepidation, knowing that he would be pitting his wits against county stalwarts once again, and then, if selected for the tourist match, some of the leading international players.

Charles Townsend

Townsend's physique was also very slender – Wisden's correspondent wrote how 'at first sight, Townsend's slight build gives the impression of being scarcely strong enough to stand the fatigue of a three day match'. But the county selectors had faith in him, especially as the college wicket was likely to assist the spinners, so when the Gloucestershire side were practising before the match with Somerset, Townsend got plenty of advice from his colleagues. 'Just toss the ball up,' said one, while another chipped in 'Don't be afraid if they try to hit you through the chapel window.'

The callow youth dutifully followed these instructions in the first innings, but he met with little success at first, so other bowlers were given preference when Somerset batted again on the second afternoon, eager to build on their first innings lead and set Gloucestershire a challenging target on the final day. Lionel Palairet led the charge with 72, whilst Vernon Hill, another renowned hitter, hit a breezy 29 as Somerset duly built up a sizeable advantage.

Sammy Woods must have fancied his chances of continuing the run spree as the Gloucestershire

The crowd in front of the pavilion at the Cheltenham Cricket Festival of 1908 when Gloucestershire played Yorkshire.

captain turned to Townsend once more as the bowlers started to tire. Sensing that he had nothing to lose, Townsend gave the ball plenty of flight, and in the space of a remarkable five minutes wrote his name into cricket's record books as, together with wicketkeeper and fellow Old Cliftonian William Brain, he recorded the only instance in first-class cricket of a hat-trick with all three batsmen dismissed stumped in consecutive balls.

Arthur Newton, the visitors' free-hitting wicketkeeper was the first to be stumped as he danced down the wicket to the schoolboy spinner. George Nichols, who had previously played as an amateur for Gloucestershire before turning professional and joining Somerset, went down the track to his first ball, missed and was stumped, before Edwin Tyler attempted something similar, only to become Brain's third victim in so many balls.

There was plenty of backslapping for Townsend, who was now beaming with delight after his remarkable hat-trick. The youngster went on to take 655 wickets for Gloucestershire; in 1898 he became the county's first player to perform the double of 1,000 runs and 100 wickets in a season, fully justifying the faith W.G. and others had in him.

While Townsend had a meteoric rise to fame, William Brain disappeared soon afterwards from the first-class scene. 1893 was his only season as Gloucestershire's wicketkeeper as he opted to follow a career with his family's brewery in Cardiff, and followed his elder brother Joseph, who had also played for Gloucestershire, across the Severn to South Wales. William duly became the regular wicketkeeper in Glamorgan's side, as the Welsh county entered the Minor County Championship under Joseph Brain's leadership in 1897. William eventually retired in 1908 before becoming chairman of Brain's Brewery in 1914.

SOMERSET

Played at Cheltenham College on 14th, 15th, 16th August 1893   Toss: Somerset
Somerset beat Gloucestershire by 127 runs

SOMERSET

W.C.Hedley		b Murch	8	(4)	c Brain	b Ferris	14
L.C.H.Palairet		b Roberts	27		c Painter	b Ferris	72
J.B.Challen		b Murch	14		st Brain	b W.G.Grace	30
R.C.N.Palairet	c Brain	b Roberts	16	(5)	c W.G.Grace	b Roberts	39
V.T.Hill		b Roberts	0	(6)	c Page	b Murch	29
W.N.Roe		b Roberts	75	(7)	not	out	9
H.T.Hewett *	c Page	b Murch	0	(1)	c Painter	b Murch	33
S.M.J.Woods	st Brain	b Townsend	26		c de Winton	b Townsend	22
A.E.Newton +	c de Winton	b Murch	13		st Brain	b Townsend	4
G.B.Nichols	not	out	9		st Brain	b Townsend	0
E.J.Tyler		b Ferris	1		st Brain	b Townsend	0
Extras	(b 8)		8		(b 15, lb 3)		18
TOTAL			197				270

GLOUCESTERSHIRE

R.W.Rice		c & b Tyler	0		c Roe	b Tyler	2
J.J.Ferris		b Nichols	32	(3)		b Tyler	1
W.G.Grace jnr.	c Newton	b Nichols	7	(5)		c & b Woods	14
G.S.de Winton	lbw	b Tyler	80		run	out	10
J.R.Painter	c R.C.N.Palairet	b Hedley	6	(2)	c Newton	b Woods	11
E.M.Grace *		b Hedley	0		c L.C.H.Palairet	b Tyler	28
H.V.Page	c L.C.H.Palairet	b Nichols	22			b Nichols	40
W.H.Brain +	c Woods	b Tyler	5		c Hewett	b Tyler	17
C.L.Townsend	not	out	1		c R.C.N.Palairet	b Tyler	4
W.H.Murch		b Tyler	2		c R.C.N.Palairet	b Hedley	26
F.G.Roberts	c Hill	b Tyler	1		not	out	11
Extras	(b 9, lb 1)		10		(b 10)		10
TOTAL			166				174

GLOUCESTERSHIRE	O	M	R	W	O	M	R	W
Townsend	20	3	71	1	8	1	16	4
Murch	24	5	67	4	20	2	88	2
Roberts	17	2	43	4	15	3	44	1
Ferris	2.3	1	8	1	19	2	74	2
W.G.Grace					12	3	30	1
SOMERSET								
Tyler	33.2	12	39	5	36	10	71	5
Woods	13	2	32	0	21	4	46	2
Nichols	35	15	48	3	10	4	24	1
Hedley	23	8	37	2	7.2	2	23	1

FALL OF WICKETS

	S	G	S	G
	1st	1st	2nd	2nd
1st	10	0	58	2
2nd	32	31	122	15
3rd	58	51	143	19
4th	58	68	174	37
5th	71	68	219	47
6th	74	140	233	82
7th	118	162	265	127
8th	153	162	270	131
9th	186	164	270	144
10th	197	166	270	174

Umpires: J.Street and S.Talboys

Gloucestershire's ranks have been decorated by many fine batsmen, with brutal hitting powers, but none can claim to have been more explosive than Gilbert Laird Jessop, the son of a Cheltenham surgeon who in 1903 struck a double century in just two hours – at the time the fastest ever recorded – against Sussex at Hove.

The game began on the Monday of the Whitsun Bank Holiday, and the twenty-nine-year-old's remarkable assault delighted the 7,000 or so spectators who packed themselves into the intimate County Ground at Hove. Jessop arrived at the crease ten minutes before lunch with Gloucestershire on 94 for 3, and in the couple of overs before the interval, he quietly played himself in. The break rather galvanised the Sussex bowlers, who quickly claimed two more wickets straight afterwards, but whatever thoughts they may have held of quickly polishing off the batting, and then putting their

'The Croucher' Gilbert Jessop

21

feet up for the rest of the day, were quickly dispelled as Jessop joined forces with wicketkeeper Jack Board, and the pair then shared a whirlwind partnership of 320 in the space of two-and-a-half hours.

Jessop raced to his half-century in thirty-two minutes, before reaching three figures just thirty-eight minutes later. However, he might not have reached his century had Francis Marlow held onto a sharp chance standing at mid-on when Jessop was on 98. This proved to be Jessop's only mistake and the Sussex fielder was left to rue his luck as the Gloucestershire batsman doubled his score in the space of the next fifty minutes. Time and again, Jessop drove the ball along the ground with awesome power and timing, as well as playing a mix of deft and quite audacious cuts against the Sussex spinners, who became increasingly frustrated by his daring strokes.

George Cox, the Sussex stalwart later recalled, 'as Jessop put your best ball to the boundary – one could not but admire that wonderful footwork combined with eye and wristwork. Once when he got in, there seemed no method of shifting him. I remember Joe Vine coming to me saying "How can you bowl to a blighter who cuts you from outside the leg peg?" One felt he wouldn't possibly continue taking such risks in batting without sooner or later making a mistake. Unfortunately for the bowler, it was too often later!'

Jessop sailed on past 200, and his previous career-best of 233, and for a while it looked as if he might record an amazing triple hundred. But his great innings eventually ended, thanks to a remarkable catch by Ranjitsinhji, who, diving one-handed, clung on to a low skimming catch fielding at long-off in front of the South Stand. Ranji's catch was later described by C.B. Fry as the most marvellous he ever saw, and at a time when diving catches in the outfield were very unusual, it seemed fitting that something special should end Jessop's record-breaking display.

In all, Jessop scored 286 out of 355 in just 175 minutes at the crease, hitting 43 fours, 8 threes, 28 twos and just 34 singles. Through his efforts, Gloucestershire were able to build a sizeable total from which their bowlers forced the follow-on. The wicket, which had appeared quite docile during Jessop's blitz, became more spiteful after a spell of rain, and on the final day, the visitors looked as though they would win. But 'Ranji' defied the Gloucestershire attack, and with the wicket drying out and easing, his unbeaten 162 saw his side to safety.

SUSSEX v GLOUCESTERSHIRE

Played at Hove on 1st, 2nd, 3rd June 1903
Match Drawn

Toss: Gloucestershire

GLOUCESTERSHIRE

S.A.P.Kitcat		b Cox	36
H.Wrathall	c Butt	b Relf	0
W.H.Hale	c Marlow	b Vine	42
T.Langdon		c & b Cox	13
G.L.Jessop *	c Ranjitsinhji	b Killick	286
L.D.Brownlee		b Cox	0
J.H.Board +		b Killick	71
H.J.Huggins	c Butt	b Killick	9
A.S.Nott	c Tate	b Cox	8
E.G.Dennett	lbw	b Killick	1
F.G.Roberts	not	out	0
Extras	(b 1, lb 10, w 5)		16

TOTAL			482

SUSSEX

C.B.Fry	c Jessop	b Dennett	83		b Roberts	6
J.Vine		b Huggins	29	lbw	b Dennett	4
E.H.Killick	c Hale	b Dennett	10	c Dennett	b Brownlee	33
K.S.Ranjitsinhji *		b Huggins	0	not	out	162
A.E.Relf	c Board	b Huggins	7		b Kitcat	50
C.L.A.Smith	c Jessop	b Dennett	34	not	out	54
H.R.Butt +	c Hale	b Dennett	4			
G.R.Cox		b Huggins	0			
F.W.Marlow	c Roberts	b Jessop	46			
C.H.G.Bland	c Dennett	b Roberts	4			
F.W.Tate	not	out	29			
Extras	(b 9, lb 9, w 1, nb 1)		20	(b 12, lb 1, w 2, nb 1)		16
			---			---
TOTAL			266	(for 4 wkts)		325

SUSSEX	O	M	R	W	O	M	R	W
Relf	22	8	65	1				
Tate	24	2	100	0				
Bland	17	7	44	0				
Cox	25.5	2	129	4				
Vine	21	6	80	1				
Marlow	5	0	31	0				
Killick	9	3	17	4				
GLOUCESTERSHIRE								
Roberts	23	8	35	1	14	3	30	1
Huggins	32	13	76	4	18	10	27	0
Dennett	45	18	93	4	22	8	50	1
Nott	8	1	24	0	4	0	26	0
Jessop	7.3	4	18	1	6	1	31	0
Brownlee					21	5	75	1
Kitcat					5	2	17	1
Langdon					9	1	53	0

FALL OF WICKETS

	G	S	S
	1st	1st	2nd
1st	0	120	6
2nd	68	127	10
3rd	94	131	77
4th	108	131	186
5th	129	143	
6th	449	148	
7th	473	149	
8th	475	191	
9th	480	200	
10th	482	266	

Umpires: T.Mycroft and C.E.Richardson

SOMERSET

Gilbert Jessop played many match-winning innings for Gloucestershire. Ferocious in their execution, they were quite remarkable in their construction, especially given the fact that Jessop had been entirely self-taught as a batsman, and as a consequence, possessed a rather unique, if ungainly, stance at the wicket. Although 'The Croucher' was a rather apt description, Jessop hated this sobriquet, as well as other rather ungenerous suggestions that he was just a cultivated slogger. Those who witnessed his demolition of the Somerset bowlers at Bristol in 1904 were left in no doubt about his brilliance and craft as a batsman.

After a fine display from bowlers George Dennett and Harry Huggins, Gloucestershire had, what on paper, seemed to be a straightforward task of scoring 298 to win on the final day. They made a promising start, but after a rain break for fifty minutes, they fell behind the clock, and lost a couple of wickets. Realising that Jessop's wicket was the prized scalp, the overs shortly before lunch saw some cat-and-mouse play, as the Somerset bowlers tried to tempt the Gloucestershire captain into making a rash stroke.

The final over before the interval was bowled by Len Braund, the canny Somerset leg-spinner who had dismissed Jessop in the first innings. After watching Jessop unfurl some attacking shots, Braund hoped Jessop would miscue another catch, and positioned several men deep on the leg side, but left the off side practically deserted, apart from a deep cover-point. He then proceeded to bowl a series of well-flighted balls, pitching outside leg stump. But Jessop was not going to fall into the cunning trap, and to the first, he came down the wicket and punched the ball past cover for four. The second was cut past cover-point to the fence for another boundary, before the third was deposited on the half-volley high for six into the tennis courts alongside the pavilion.

Gilbert Jessop (left) on the outfield at Hove in 1913.

Len Braund

In all of his county career, Braund had never been treated with such contempt, so in an attempt to stifle Jessop he moved an extra man across to the off side and then delivered the next ball with less air and more pace down the leg side. But Jessop was in no mood for containment, and after hopping back, he cut it just backward of point for another four to Braund's complete dismay. So it was back to plan 'A' for the next delivery, with another well-flighted topspinner, hoping this time that Jessop would over-reach himself. But Jessop dispatched it past cover-point for another boundary, to make it 22 from the first five balls of the over.

A hush then descended over the Ashley Down ground as the home crowd drew breath in anticipation of what Jessop would do to the final ball before lunch. For his part, Jessop remained calm, hitching up his trousers as Braund looked quizzically at his captain Sammy Woods in the vain hope of a word of advice. None was forthcoming as Jessop took strike to what turned out to be a

SOMERSET

ball short of a length. Like a spring uncoiling, Jessop leaped down the wicket and sent the ball high over the boundary fence for another six, to the accompaniment of loud cheers and rapturous applause from the crowd who had witnessed a record 28 runs in an over.

In the space of ten minutes, Jessop had hit 45 runs, and during the luncheon interval, news quickly spread into the city of Jessop's record-breaking feat. The crowd had noticeably swelled by the time play resumed, and the battle between Braund and Jessop continued. To the first over, Jessop was content to strike 2 fours and 2 twos, taking his tally to a remarkable 57 in the space of just a quarter of an hour, but just as people continued to pour through the gates, hoping to see more audacious hitting from Jessop, he edged Ernie Robson into Braund's hands at slip.

He departed to a standing ovation and wild cheers, as his 61 out of 73 in just twenty-four minutes, had put the Gloucestershire side well ahead of the clock, and Somerset well and truly on the back foot. Tom Langdon then played a very sober 83 in three hours, and despite the clatter of further wickets, he ensured that Jessop's efforts were not wasted by guiding Gloucestershire home with three wickets in hand.

A 'Rip' cartoon showing the interest generated when Jessop was batting.

GLOUCESTERSHIRE v SOMERSET

Played at Bristol on 16th, 17th, 18th May 1904   Toss: Somerset
Gloucestershire beat Somerset by 3 wickets

SOMERSET

Batsman	Dismissal 1		Runs		Dismissal 2		Runs
L.C.H.Palairet	c Langdon	b Dennett	32			b Spry	166
L.C.Braund	c Dennett	b Huggins	4			b Huggins	19
A.E.Lewis	c Spry	b Dennett	47			b Huggins	7
E.Robson	c Jessop	b Dennett	4			b Langdon	60
H.Martyn +		b Huggins	0	(6)		b Huggins	10
S.M.J.Woods *		b Dennett	0	(9)		b Huggins	1
H.S.Poyntz	c Hale	b Dennett	32			b Huggins	5
F.M.Lee	not	out	17	(5)	c Sellick	b Langdon	20
F.P.Hardy	c Spry	b Dennett	8	(8)	c Hale	b Spry	13
C.H.Alison		b Dennett	5		not	out	0
A.E.C.North	c Thomas	b Dennett	6			b Huggins	0
Extras	(b 9, nb 2)		11		(b 5, lb 4)		9
TOTAL			166				310

GLOUCESTERSHIRE

Batsman	Dismissal 1		Runs		Dismissal 2		Runs
E.P.Barnett	c Martyn	b Braund	5			b Palairet	38
H.Wrathall		b North	26	(5)	c & b	Palairet	33
G.L.Jessop *	c Lee	b Braund	20	(4)	c Braund	b Robson	61
F.E.Thomas	c Braund	b North	25	(7)		b North	17
W.H.Hale	c Palairet	b Braund	0	(6)		b Braund	10
T.Langdon	lbw	b Lewis	17	(3)	not	out	83
J.H.Board +	lbw	b North	2	(9)	not	out	3
E.J.Spry	c Palairet	b North	30				
H.J.Huggins		b Braund	38	(8)	c Martyn	b North	4
A.S.Sellick	not	out	9	(2)	lbw	b Braund	44
E.G.Dennett		b Braund	0				
Extras	(b 3, lb 4)		7		(b 5)		5
TOTAL			179		(for 7 wkts)		298

GLOUCESTERSHIRE	O	M	R	W	O	M	R	W
Dennett	29.3	7	93	8	32	7	89	0
Huggins	25	9	47	2	37.5	12	111	6
Jessop	2	0	9	0				
Spry	2	0	6	0	18	2	64	2
Hale					7	2	14	0
Langdon					10	2	23	2
SOMERSET								
Lewis	9	4	17	1	8	2	15	0
Braund	29.4	4	93	5	35.4	12	117	2
North	20	6	47	4	13	6	35	2
Robson	6	3	11	0	14	2	39	1
Palairet	1	0	4	0	14	4	38	2
Woods					14	4	49	0

FALL OF WICKETS

	S	G	S	G
	1st	1st	2nd	2nd
1st	16	8	34	73
2nd	38	36	59	98
3rd	39	75	186	171
4th	62	76	220	225
5th	62	85	241	238
6th	107	87	271	281
7th	134	113	300	289
8th	148	143	310	
9th	158	179	310	
10th	166	179	310	

Umpires: W.Wright and J.Carlin

ESSEX

Four bowlers have taken ten wickets in an innings for Gloucestershire; the first man to achieve this feat was George Dennett, as he took 10/40 in an outstanding display of left-arm spin against Essex at Bristol in August 1906. After a brief spell as a professional in Scotland, he had moved to take up an appointment the Bristol area, and was spotted by Gilbert Jessop. He subsequently became one of the bulwarks of the county's attack, and in his first-class career between 1903 and 1926, Dennett took 2,083 wickets at a fraction under 20 runs apiece.

With a high and quick action, Dennett had a deceptive loop, and for the batsman, a slightly disconcerting way of tilting his head to the left as he released the ball, making it seem he was watching the ball come out of his hand. His high action meant that he could also extract steep bounce from even the most benign of surfaces, and as in this classic match, he frequently took the new ball.

Dennett was one of the most difficult bowlers to face on the county circuit either side of the First World War. Once on a roll, he was almost unplayable, and as he proved in this game, his skilful variations gave new batsmen no time to settle in. With a mix of cunning and guile, Dennett soon sent the opposition batsmen back to the pavilion, especially the brightly-capped amateurs on their summer vacations, who often seemed somewhat foolishly intent on proving to their professional colleagues that the spinner could be hit for runs, only to perish with an inelegant swipe and to return rather shamefaced, but no doubt a little wiser, back to the dressing rooms.

On no less than fifty-seven occasions, Dennett took ten wickets in a match, and in this contest against Essex, his tally was fifteen victims. The visitors batted first but were hustled out by Dennett and his new-ball partner Fred Roberts for 84 shortly after lunch. None of the Essex men were comfortable facing him, and with the Gloucestershire fielders excelling themselves, wickets fell at regular intervals as the batsmen unwisely tried to hit their way out of trouble. Leigh Brownlee took three fine catches, while Jack Board made a sharp and almost nonchalant stumping as Walter Turner unwisely danced down the wicket.

Although not a true wicket, run-scoring was perfectly possible as Gloucestershire proved during the afternoon session, as they

Gilbert Jessop playing a rare forward defensive stroke.

```
                        GLOUCESTERSHIRE v ESSEX

Played at Bristol on 6th, 7th August 1906              Toss: Essex
Gloucestershire beat Essex by 9 wickets

                               ESSEX
F.L.Fane          c Jessop    b Dennett   11              b Roberts     2
J.W.H.T.Douglas * b Dennett   14          c Townsend    b Dennett     25
P.A.Perrin        c Brownlee  b Dennett   22          st Board      b Dennett      1
C.P.McGahey       c Brownlee  b Dennett   17          st Board      b Dennett      8
W.M.F.Turner      st Board    b Dennett    0          c Goodwin     b Dennett     37
F.H.Gillingham    c Spry      b Dennett    4 ( 7) c Thomas     b Dennett     20
A.J.Turner        c Thomas    b Dennett    3 (10)         lbw  b Roberts      9
W.Reeves          c Brownlee  b Dennett    4 ( 9)              b Roberts      7
C.P.Buckenham        lbw      b Dennett    5 ( 8)         not         out      4
A.E.Russell +        not         out      0 ( 6)              b Roberts      4
W.Mead            c Goodwin   b Dennett    2          c Sewell      b Roberts      0
     Extras       (lb 2)                                 (b 6, lb 4)           10
                                          ---                                  ---
     TOTAL                                 84                                  127

                          GLOUCESTERSHIRE
C.O.H.Sewell      st Russell  b Mead      21              b Douglas    14
E.P.Barnett                   b Reeves    17              not        out       20
G.L.Jessop *                c & b Douglas 75
A.F.M.Townsend    c Fane      b Mead      23
J.H.Board +          lbw      b Douglas    0
F.E.Thomas                    b Douglas    4
L.D.Brownlee                  b Mead       6 ( 3)        not        out        5
H.S.Goodwin       c McGahey   b Douglas    6
F.B.Roberts                   b Reeves    10
E.J.Spry          c Reeves    b Douglas    6
E.G.Dennett          not         out       0
     Extras       (b 4, lb 1)              5
                                          ---                                  ---
     TOTAL                                173          (for 1 wkt)             39

GLOUCESTERSHIRE   O     M    R    W      O     M    R    W    FALL OF WICKETS
Dennett         19.4    7   40   10     31    12   48    5            E    G    E    G
Roberts         19      8   42    0     30.2   7   69    5          1st  1st  2nd  2nd
                                                              1st    19   38   20   21
ESSEX                                                         2nd    47   38   25
Mead            19      3   72    3      4     0   12    0    3rd    47   81   40
Douglas         14      3   50    5      3.5   0   27    1    4th    47   84   47
Reeves          10      1   46    2                          5th    55   98   68
                                                             6th    70  113   96
                                                             7th    75  140  106
                                                             8th    81  163  110
                                                             9th    82  171  127
                                                            10th    84  173  127

Umpires: A.E.Clapp and F.W.Marlow
```

amassed 173 with Jessop hitting a graceful and for once quite sober 75 in an hour and a half at the crease. Before the first day was over, Essex had begun their second innings, and Dennett continued his wicket-taking spree, as Essex slumped to 63 for 4. Their resistance ended after a shade over seventy-five minutes the following morning, as Dennett and Roberts finished with 5 wickets apiece.

Dennett had match figures of 15/88 – a worthy reward after completely bamboozling the Essex batsmen. But George was a very self-effacing fellow, and as befitted someone not prone to demonstrative gestures, he quietly walked off the Bristol ground modestly doffing his cap in recognition of his outstanding feat.

Northamptonshire

10, 11, 12 June 1907 at Gloucester Spa

'Northants did little during the season of 1907 upon which either the members of the team or the supporters of the county club could look back with pride.' So wrote *Wisden's* correspondent after a season that saw Northamptonshire, who had entered the County Championship only two years before, lose twelve of their twenty games and enter the cricket record books for the lowest ever total in a county match, as Gloucestershire dismissed them for just 12.

This remarkable game took place at the somewhat unpretentious and tree-lined Spa Ground in Gloucester – the pretty parkland ground, overlooked by elegant Regency villas, had staged Championship fixtures since 1882, but it had a less than attractive reputation among county batsmen and on more than one occasion, doubts were expressed about the suitability of the Spa wicket for first-class cricket.

Rain restricted play to just fifty minutes on the opening day, and given the capricious history of the wicket, Gilbert Jessop had no hesitation in deciding to bat first. But George Thompson, the Northants fast-medium bowler, took three

quick wickets as Gloucestershire slipped to 20 for 4. On the following morning, Jessop played some expansive shots to get the scoreboard ticking over, but batting was something of a lottery as his side were soon dismissed for 60.

If the home side had found it difficult to score runs on the Spa wicket, it seemed likely that the visitors would struggle as well, but even the most diehard of Gloucestershire supporters would not have predicted what happened next, as Northants were dismissed in just forty minutes for the lowest ever total in Championship history.

George Dennett (above) was virtually unplayable, extracting prodigious turn and lavish bounce, and he claimed a hat-trick dismissing Roger Hawtin, Robert Beasley and Walter Buswell in successive balls. In fact, it should have been four in four had Harry Wrathall not dropped Billy East off the next delivery. But East did not last long as he soon became another stumping victim for Jack Board, before Jessop claimed the final two wickets as Northants were dismissed for 12. With his thirty-six deliveries, Dennett had claimed 8/9 in an astonishing display of controlled, and at times vicious, spin bowling.

The wickets continued to fall, although with slightly less speed, when Gloucestershire batted again, and for the second time in the game, Jessop's bold stroke-play helped his side out of difficulty. His furious blows allowed the home team to secure a lead of 136, but this became purely an academic target as once again, Dennett's spin caused complete mayhem among Northants' ranks. The left-arm spinner took a further 7 wickets as the visitors subsided to 40 for 7 at the close of an eventful day that had seen no less than 33 wickets fall for the addition of just 180 runs.

GLOUCESTERSHIRE v NORTHAMPTONSHIRE

Played at Gloucester Spa on 10th, 11th, 12th June 1907   Toss: Gloucestershire
Match Drawn

GLOUCESTERSHIRE

Batsman		First innings				Second innings	
E.P.Barnett	lbw	b Thompson	3 (7)			b East	0
H.Wrathall		b Thompson	4 (3)			b Thompson	7
J.H.Board +		b Thompson	3 (4)		lbw	b Thompson	5
M.G.Salter	c Buswell	b East	3 (6)		c &	b East	3
G.L.Jessop *		b East	22	c Hawtin		b East	24
R.T.H.Mackenzie		b East	0 (1)	c King		b East	21
T.Langdon		b East	4 (2)		lbw	b Thompson	4
H.J.Huggins	c Crosse	b East	8	c Buswell		b East	3
E.J.Spry	lbw	b Thompson	6			b East	4
C.W.L.Parker	not	out	2		not	out	8
E.G.Dennett	c Pool	b Thompson	0			b East	0
Extras	(b 2, lb 3)		5	(b 9)			9
TOTAL			60				88

NORTHAMPTONSHIRE

Batsman		First innings				Second innings	
E.M.Crosse *	c Board	b Dennett	4		c & b	Dennett	0
M.Cox	lbw	b Dennett	2	c Barnett		b Dennett	12
C.J.T.Pool	c Spry	b Dennett	4 (4)	st Board		b Dennett	9
W.A.Buswell +	st Board	b Dennett	1 (7)	c Langdon		b Dennett	0
L.T.Driffield		b Dennett	0				
G.J.Thompson		b Dennett	0 (5)		not	out	5
R.W.R.Hawtin	lbw	b Dennett	0 (3)		lbw	b Dennett	8
W.East	st Board	b Dennett	0		lbw	b Dennett	2
R.N.Beasley		b Jessop	1 (6)			b Dennett	0
S.King	not	out	0 (9)		not	out	1
W.Wells	c Parker	b Jessop	0				
Extras				(b 2, lb 1)			3
TOTAL			12	(for 7 wkts)			40

NORTHAMPTONSHIRE	O	M	R	W	O	M	R	W
Thompson	16.5	7	29	5	15	2	43	3
East	16	5	26	5	14.2	4	36	7
GLOUCESTERSHIRE								
Dennett	6	1	9	8	15	8	12	7
Jessop	5.3	4	3	2	10	3	20	0
Parker					5	2	5	0

FALL OF WICKETS

	G 1st	N 1st	G 2nd	N 2nd
1st	4	6	17	4
2nd	11	10	35	17
3rd	14	11	35	20
4th	20	11	52	25
5th	20	11	57	30
6th	32	11	57	35
7th	45	11	68	35
8th	58	12	80	
9th	60	12	85	
10th	60	12	88	

Umpires: A.Millward and J.E.West

Dennett's day had seen him claim 15/21 in 21 overs, and as he headed home from the Spa Ground he must have given more than just a passing thought about the prospect of picking up all 10 wickets in an innings once again. But the weather had the final say, as heavy rain washed out the third day's play, allowing Northants to escape from their hopeless position with a draw.

MIDDLESEX

1909 was a sorry summer for Gloucestershire – in 22 matches they only recorded a single victory, and with 13 defeats, the club ended their worst ever season to date firmly at the bottom of the Championship table.

Gloucestershire sorely missed their captain Gilbert Jessop, who strained his back playing in the Third Test at Headingley at the start of July, and missed the second half of the season. They were also without Charles Townsend, who by now was pursuing a legal career, and as a result only appeared sporadically for the county. He played against the touring Australians at Cheltenham and struck a fine century inside two hours, but this was a rare moment of sunshine in what was a very gloomy season for the West Country side.

For most of the summer, the Gloucestershire batting relied on Tom Langdon, Fred Roberts and Jack Board, and when they failed, the weaknesses of the largely amateur middle order were cruelly exposed, and as a consequence, they rarely posted a sizeable total. Things steadily went from bad to worse and then culminated in an ignominious defeat in just one day against Middlesex at Bristol – the first and only time Gloucestershire had been beaten inside a day.

The contest began in dramatic fashion as Gloucestershire were dismissed in just over an hour's play for 33, with none of their batsmen reaching double figures. Frank Tarrant, the Australian all-rounder, ripped the heart out of the Gloucestershire batting with his left-arm cutters, and then set about the home team's bowling with an unbeaten half-century.

The visitors also found batting quite difficult on the Bristol wicket, but Tarrant remained steadfast as wickets fell around him. On occasions, the Australian had been criticised for adopting a too cautious approach, but on this particular day, Middlesex were very grateful for his careful occupation of the crease, which spanned ninety minutes, and saw him give just one difficult chance. But his colleagues were less fortunate, as the left-arm spin of George Dennett and the right-arm seam of Harry Huggins (right) dismissed Middlesex for 145.

Having been on the field throughout, Tarrant could have been excused for wanting a breather, but no sooner had the Gloucestershire openers taken guard, than he was rolling up his sleeves again and running in to bowl. It continued to be a good day for him as he took five of the first

```
                    GLOUCESTERSHIRE v MIDDLESEX

Played at Bristol on 26th August 1909                Toss: Gloucestershire
Middlesex beat Gloucestershire by an innings and 31 runs


                           GLOUCESTERSHIRE
C.S.Barnett           c & b Hearne      9          run          out         6
J.H.Board +               b Tarrant     7                  c & b Tarrant   14
T.Langdon       lbw       b Tarrant     2      st Murrell    b Tarrant      0
W.M.Brownlee              b Hearne      2      c Mignon      b Tarrant      0
W.E.Meyer                b Tarrant     3      st Murrell    b Tarrant      0
R.T.Godsell     c Mignon   b Tarrant    4           lbw       b Tarrant      0
A.D.Imlay       st Murrell b Tarrant    0      c Tarrant     b Hearne       6
W.S.A.Brown *   lbw        b Tarrant    0           lbw       b Tarrant     32
H.J.Huggins     st Murrell b Hearne     0 (10) c Hearne      b Wells        5
C.W.L.Parker    c Hendren  b Tarrant    0 (11)     not          out         0
E.G.Dennett         not       out       1 ( 9)          c & b Wells         8
     Extras     (b 4, lb 1)             5          (b 7, lb 2, nb 1)       10
                                       ---                                 ---
     TOTAL                              33                                  81

                            MIDDLESEX
J.Douglas             c & b Dennett     6
F.A.Tarrant           not     out      55
E.H.Hendren     c Godsell   b Dennett  12
G.L.Hebden      lbw         b Parker    0
H.R.Murrell +               b Parker   22
A.E.Trott       c Brownlee  b Dennett  18
H.A.Bates                   b Huggins  10
C.M.Wells *                 b Huggins   0
R.E.More                    b Huggins   7
J.T.Hearne                  b Dennett   5
E.Mignon        c Meyer     b Huggins   6
     Extras     (b 2, lb 1, nb 1)       4
                                       ---
     TOTAL                             145

MIDDLESEX       O     M    R    W     O    M    R    W      FALL OF WICKETS
Tarrant         11.4  3    18   7     18   1    49   6           G    M    G
Hearne          11    7    10   3     15   4    20   1          1st  1st  2nd
Wells                                 2.3  0    2    2     1st    8    ?   17
                                                          2nd    ?   29   20
GLOUCESTERSHIRE                                           3rd   19   29   20
Dennett         17    0    76   4                         4th    ?   59   20
Parker          10    2    52   2                         5th    ?   80   20
Huggins         6.5   2    13   4                         6th    ?  107   21
                                                         7th   32  107   45
                                                         8th   32  125    ?
                                                         9th   32  135    ?
                                                        10th   33  145   81


Umpires: W.A.J.West and B.W.Mason
```

six wickets to fall as for the second time in the space of a few hours, the Gloucestershire batting disintegrated.

William Brown briefly showed that the Middlesex bowling could be attacked and he struck a quick-fire 32 before being the thirteenth victim of the day for Tarrant. Soon afterwards, Colin Wells claimed the wicket of Huggins to wrap up the match that had spanned just 92 overs and had dramatically, inside a single day's play, brought the curtain down on a summer that most of the West Country cricketers would sooner forget.

SOMERSET

Professional sport is full of 'ifs' and 'maybes', and one of the greatest imponderables in Gloucestershire cricket is how many more runs might Charles Townsend have scored for the county if from 1900 he had played for them on a regular basis.

In his first-class career between 1893 and 1922, he made 7,754 runs in 161 appearances, but from the turn of the century, he turned this attention to the legal world, initially acting as a solicitor, and then the Official Receiver for Stockton-on-Tees. Many watchers of Gloucestershire cricket believe that had Townsend opted to regularly play county cricket, he would have scored over 20,000 runs, and might even have passed W.G. Grace's aggregate of 22,808 runs for the club.

Despite his other interests, he remained an active supporter of the county club, and helped from afar with fund-raising, but his appearances for Gloucestershire gradually became few and far between. Even though he lacked match practice and had more than a few grey hairs, Townsend showed in his fleeting appearances that he had lost nothing of his abilities as a batsman, to the

JC White - Somerset's canny spinner

Alf Dipper the perfect foil to Townsend's hitting.

delight, and perhaps a bit of infuriation as well, of the county's supporters, who must have longed that he could have played more frequently.

An example came against Somerset at Bristol over the August Bank Holiday of 1920, where Townsend played a quite remarkable match-winning innings. He enjoyed appearing in these local derbies and the presence of the forty-three year old in the Gloucestershire side helped to swell the crowd, who were eager to see the batting maestro in action again. They had to wait though until the final afternoon, and had to endure watching Somerset gain a sizeable and rather embarrassing first innings lead as Gloucestershire were dismissed for just 22 – the lowest ever total in their history.

Frederic Waldock, the Ceylonese left-hander, and the dapper and stylish Jack MacBryan saw Somerset to what appeared to be at first a modest first innings total of 169, with Gloucestershire spinners George Dennett and Charlie Parker sharing eight wickets between them. Jack White, the ruddy-faced and taciturn left-arm spinner, then silenced the quite sizeable holiday crowd with an extraordinary spell of 7/10 in just nine overs.

'Farmer' White was not a huge spinner of the ball, and his chief weapon was clever flight. It proved to be sufficient to hustle out the Gloucestershire batsmen who in the space of 18 overs were dismissed for 22. Alf Dipper and Percy Williams were joint-top scorers with 5 runs apiece, and as each wicket quickly fell, an eerie silence came over the partisan Bristol crowd who could hardly believe what they were witnessing. Townsend was equally shocked at his side's alarming demise,

SOMERSET

John Daniell, the Somerset captain.

and as he fielded during Somerset's second innings, he vowed to avenge his team's humiliation. He had to wait though until John Daniell, the Somerset captain, felt the time was right to declare.

As it turned out, Daniell made the decision quite early on the final day, primarily to allow his bowlers enough time to bowl Gloucestershire out again. He quite rightly believed that they would put up greater resistance, but as events transpired his decision also gave Gloucestershire sufficient time to chase 274 on the final afternoon.

However, Daniell could not have taken into his calculations both the sheer brilliance of Townsend, who with an air of disdain, completely took apart the Somerset attack, nor the way his bowlers, in the face of Townsend's onslaught, became almost impotent. This was not the first time in the 1920s that the Somerset side failed to force home an advantage, and for all the assertiveness and iron will of Daniell, it failed to rub off on others.

Townsend, with a wide array of cultured drives, raced to 84 in just seventy-five minutes as Gloucestershire sped to 119, before he was caught off Jim Bridges' in-swingers. The Somerset man also dismissed Townsend's opening partner Alf Dipper, who either side of the First World War had been the sheet anchor of the Gloucestershire batting. Dipper's contribution was a pugnacious 48, and he was the ideal foil for the dashing and exquisite stroke-play of Townsend, who broke the back and perhaps the heart of the Somerset bowlers.

By the time Dipper and Townsend had each departed to rapturous applause from the now-animated crowd, the target had become far more manageable, but Harry Rowlands and Harry Smith soon returned to the pavilion. However, two of Gloucestershire's military men, Percy Robinson – later to be a Lt Col – and Michael Green – who subsequently rose to the rank of Brigadier – then held their nerve and took their side closer and closer to the target. Gloucestershire eventually got home with four wickets in hand, and the Somerset players walked off the Bristol ground wondering how on earth they had contrived to lose a match that a few hours before had seemed to be theirs for the taking.

GLOUCESTERSHIRE v SOMERSET

Played at Bristol on 31st July, 2nd, 3rd August 1920   Toss: Somerset
Gloucestershire beat Somerset by 4 wickets

SOMERSET

Batsman	1st innings			2nd innings		
A.E.S.Rippon	run	out	1			
J.A.S.Jackson	c Williams	b Parker	5 (1)		b Parker	10
J.C.W.MacBryan		b Parker	38		not out	29
M.D.Lyon +	c Mills	b Dennett	12 (2)	lbw	b Parker	41
F.A.Waldock	c Williams	b Parker	45	run	out	2
M.L.Hambling	c P.G.Robinson	b Dennett	3 (4)		b Parker	1
J.Daniell *	c Williams	b Parker	34	c F.G.Robinson	b Mills	24
P.A.Foy		c & b Dipper	8 (6)		b Mills	2
E.Robson	c Rowlands	b Dennett	4			
J.C.White	c F.G.Robinson	b Dennett	8 (8)		b Mills	10
J.J.Bridges	not	out	0			
Extras	(b 7, lb 3, nb 1)		11	(b 5, lb 2)		7
TOTAL			169	(for 7 wkts dec)		126

GLOUCESTERSHIRE

Batsman	1st innings			2nd innings		
C.L.Townsend	lbw	b Robson	4	c Robson	b Bridges	84
A.E.Dipper	c Daniell	b White	5		b Bridges	48
W.H.Rowlands		b Robson	0	c MacBryan	b White	7
H.Smith	c Daniell	b White	1	c White	b Robson	1
P.G.Robinson		c & b White	2	c Waldock	b Robson	37
M.A.Green	c MacBryan	b White	3	not	out	32
F.G.Robinson *+	c Daniell	b White	0		b Bridges	28
P.F.C.Williams		b Robson	5	not	out	14
P.T.Mills	st Lyon	b White	0			
C.W.L.Parker		c & b White	2			
E.G.Dennett	not	out	0			
Extras				(b 18, lb 7)		25
TOTAL			22	(for 6 wkts)		276

GLOUCESTERSHIRE	O	M	R	W	O	M	R	W
Dennett	38.5	16	68	4	15	4	43	0
Parker	39	20	58	4	19	5	41	3
Dipper	7	2	19	1				
Mills	6	2	13	0	13.3	2	35	3

SOMERSET	O	M	R	W	O	M	R	W
Robson	9	4	12	3	23	3	68	2
White	9	4	10	7	25	7	65	1
Bridges					20	4	74	3
Foy					4	0	24	0
Hambling					8	3	20	0

FALL OF WICKETS

	S	G	S	G
	1st	1st	2nd	2nd
1st	5	5	51	119
2nd	6	9	54	132
3rd	22	9	56	139
4th	100	12	66	181
5th	105	13	69	197
6th	105	13	102	243
7th	149	16	126	
8th	158	16		
9th	167	20		
10th	169	22		

Umpires: A.E.Street and J.Blake

YORKSHIRE

As befitted a man who took over 3,000 wickets, Charlie Parker (opposite) was a wise old fox. When granted a benefit in 1922, the left-arm spinner had little hesitation in choosing the game against Yorkshire as the one from which he could take the match receipts. At the time, the Yorkshire side were among the strongest in the country, with many household names, including Percy Holmes and Herbert Sutcliffe, England's finest pair of opening batsmen. Parker knew that their visit to the West Country would, given fine weather, draw a good crowd. The match was initially one of two allocated to Clifton College, and in a show of support to both Gloucestershire and Parker, Charles Townsend, who by now had more than an eye on retirement, made himself available for what could have been a final innings on the College Ground that had launched his career.

But the two fixtures could not be fitted into the college vacation, so the games were switched to the Fry's Ground. To the relief of Parker, Townsend confirmed his availability, but as the players gathered at the Bristol ground on the morning of 9 August it looked as if the elements were conspiring against the Gloucestershire man. Rain prevented any play until three o'clock, and then heavy cloud and poor light meant an early finish with Gloucestershire on 92 for 4.

However, the weather was set fair on the second day, and a large crowd were present as Gloucestershire's innings resumed, although many were eagerly anticipating the start of the Yorkshire innings. The prospect of seeing Charlie Parker pit his wiles against some of England's premier batsmen was a mouth-watering one, and neither Parker, or the spectators were to be disappointed as he produced one of the finest spells in his illustrious career.

In his first six overs, Parker dismissed the top four men in the Yorkshire side, and with the final ball of his seventh over he clean bowled Norman Kilner to take his tally to five. The first ball of his next over rattled the stumps again, but Parker had overstepped the crease and was called for a no-ball. However, Parker calmly went back to his mark, and then clean bowled Macauley, Dolphin and Waddington in successive deliveries.

It was the first hat-trick of his wonderful career, and including the no-ball, he had hit the stumps five times in succession. Yorkshire's first innings lasted just seventy minutes, and after taking the final wicket, Parker departed to a standing ovation, having taken 9/36 in one of the most remarkable spells of bowling ever seen in a county match.

But Yorkshire immediately struck back, with Wilfred Rhodes taking five wickets as Gloucestershire subsided in the late afternoon. Within two hours their resistance was over, with only Alf Dipper, in typically determined mood, getting into double figures, as Gloucestershire finished 164 runs ahead. Little went Gloucestershire's way on the final morning, as half-chances

```
                        GLOUCESTERSHIRE v YORKSHIRE

Played at Bristol on 9th, 10th, 11th August 1922        Toss: Gloucestershire
Yorkshire beat Gloucestershire by 6 wickets


                              GLOUCESTERSHIRE
C.L.Townsend               b Waddington    19                b Rhodes         3
A.E.Dipper       c Waddington b R.Kilner   54                b Rhodes        16
H.Smith +        c Dolphin  b Macaulay      4        lbw     b Rhodes         7
B.H.Lyon         c Oldroyd  b Waddington    2        lbw     b Waddington     0
M.A.Green                  b R.Kilner      15        run       out            9
P.F.C.Williams *           b R.Kilner      19     st Dolphin b Rhodes         7
F.G.Robinson     c Oldroyd  b Wilson        8                b Rhodes         4
P.T.Mills                  b Rhodes        17     c Robinson b Wilson         2
C.W.L.Parker     c Rhodes   b Macaulay      7        not       out            2
E.G.Dennett      c Rhodes   b Macaulay      7        run       out            1
J.G.W.T.Bessant     not        out          9     c Macaulay b Wilson         1
     Extras       (b 4, lb 4, nb 3)        11       (b 2, lb 3, nb 1)         6
                                          ---                               ---
     TOTAL                                172                                58


                                YORKSHIRE
P.Holmes         c Smith    b Parker        0                b Mills          6
H.Sutcliffe        lbw      b Parker       11                b Mills         17
E.Oldroyd          lbw      b Parker        0        not       out           63
R.Kilner                    b Parker       14                b Parker         0
W.Rhodes           lbw      b Mills        12     c Bessant  b Parker        22
E.Robinson                  b Parker        1        not       out           39
N.Kilner                    b Parker        5
G.G.Macaulay                b Parker        8
A.Dolphin +                 b Parker        0
A.Waddington                b Parker        0
E.R.Wilson *        not        out         13
     Extras       (b 1, nb 1)               2       (b 12, lb 8)             20
                                          ---                               ---
     TOTAL                                 66       (for 4 wkts)            167


YORKSHIRE         O    M    R    W     O    M    R    W      FALL OF WICKETS
Waddington       21    6   39    2     5    2    8    1        G    Y    G    Y
Robinson          7    3   17    0                          1st  1st  2nd  2nd
Macaulay         25    7   48    3                     1st    31    0   12   19
R.Kilner         27   14   26    3     3    0   13    0     2nd    38    0   21   44
Wilson           18    9   16    1  11.1    7    7    2     3rd    45   26   22   45
Rhodes            8    4   15    1    20   11   24    5     4th    80   27   32   71
                                                           5th   114   39   41
GLOUCESTERSHIRE                                            6th   129   44   45
Parker         10.2    2   36    9    35   17   46    2     7th   129   45   52
Mills            10    2   28    1    38   19   45    2     8th   152   45   52
Dennett                               11    3   30    0     9th   156   45   57
Bessant                                7    3   26    0    10th   172   66   58

Umpires: W.A.J.West and W.Phillips
```

were spilled and edges dropped short of the eager fielders, and when Parker took his second wicket, Yorkshire were 71 for 4.

Any thoughts of the spinner making further headway through the Yorkshire batting were soon dispelled, as Edgar Oldroyd and Emmott Robinson shared a watchful and unbeaten partnership of 96 to see the visitors home. Parker was over a thousand pounds richer after this fine duel, but how he would have loved a Gloucestershire victory and a chance to prove that his bowling was more than the equal of the cream of England's batting talent.

In 1920 Sir Foster Robinson, the Gloucestershire captain, had received a letter from the headmaster of Cirencester Grammar School, outlining the magnificent feats of a schoolboy who had struck an unbeaten 365 in a house match. The youngster was none other than Wally Hammond, and supporters of both Gloucestershire and England will forever be grateful, both to the headmaster for writing the letter, and to Robinson for acting on his advice and inviting the youngster for a trial.

Hammond went on to become one of the greatest batsmen ever to play for the county and in August 1924 at the Greenbank ground in Bristol he played his first great innings, with an unbeaten 174 on a deteriorating wicket against Middlesex: a measure of his prodigious talents was that the next highest score was 42.

Middlesex had arrived at the ground, owned by Messrs H.J. Packer and Co., the famous chocolate manufacturers, knowing that victory over the West Country side would secure the county title. The mood in their camp was high as they had just beaten Nottinghamshire after having themselves been forced to follow-on, and they left few people in any doubt about their desire to inflict a heavy defeat on Gloucestershire.

Before lunch on the first day, it looked as if their words would come true as Gloucestershire were dismissed inside seventy-five minutes for just 31, and as the first two Middlesex batsmen strode to the wicket, some of the other visitors began planning their victory celebrations. But they had reckoned without Charlie Parker who weaved his magic with 7/30 in sixty-one balls, including a hat-trick, while Hammond's medium-pace also claimed two wickets as Middlesex were brought back down to earth by only gaining a lead of 43.

F.T. Mann - the Middlesex captain.

Above, left: D.C. Robinson: the Gloucestershire wicket-keeper.

Above, right: Hammond walking to the wicket almost with a regal air.

After the clatter of 20 wickets on Saturday, most people expected the bowlers to have another field day when play resumed on Monday morning. But Hammond dispelled these thoughts and put aside his recent disappointments and a dip in his form that had seen the precocious batsman bag a pair against Worcestershire at Cheltenham. These events had weighed heavily on his mind, so before the second innings against Middlesex the young tyro received a few words of advice from his colleagues. 'Just go out and play your own game,' said one, while Parker, in his typically frank way chipped in 'Remind those cocky bastards from Lord's just what you can do.'

Whatever fickle demons lay in the wicket, Hammond was the master of them, as well as every bowler, either fast or slow, that Middlesex turned to in a vain attempt to restrict his thrilling stroke-play. In a shade under four hours, Hammond struck a majestic 174 with a six and 21 fours. Bev Lyon and later Douglas Robinson hung around for a while to offer valiant support, but it was largely a one-man show as Hammond reached a faultless century on a wicket where nobody else had reached fifty. On 137 he gave the first of two sharp chances, but he survived both and went on past 150 before Frank Mann declared to leave the visitors a tricky target of 252 on the final afternoon.

After Hammond's glorious display, the visitors felt that attack was the best form of defence, and knowing that a victory was essential, they began a bold victory bid with their top order soon putting

41

MIDDLESEX

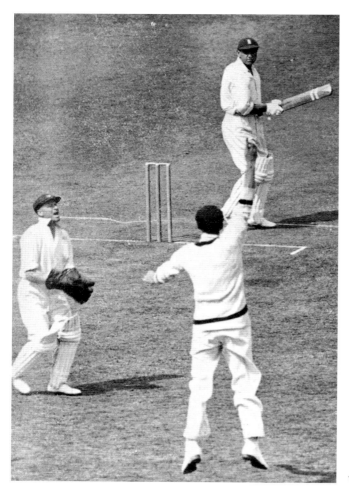

Wally Hammond is out!

them ahead of the clock. For a while it looked as if the visitors might pull off an audacious victory, but Charlie Parker put a brake on their progress, and then started to work through their batting. He had little time for some of the snobbery shown by a few of the Middlesex amateurs, so he had a wicked glint in his eye as wickets started to tumble, and then much to his delight he claimed his second hat-trick of the match as the Middlesex resistance evaporated.

As the last couple of wickets fell, the mood in the Middlesex dressing room had changed from delight to dismay as the title slipped away from their grasp, and the recriminations started to fly about the state of the Greenbank wicket. Gubby Allen claimed it was quite appalling, and one of the worst he had ever seen, while some of the Middlesex team knocked loudly on the door of the room being used by Gloucestershire's secretary, eager to vent their fury on the official, who wisely decided to keep the lock on.

Whatever the rights and wrongs of the matter, there was though one thing that everyone agreed upon – Wally Hammond was a wonderful batsman.

GLOUCESTERSHIRE v MIDDLESEX

Played at Bristol Greenbank on 23rd, 25th, 26th August 1924   Toss: Gloucestershire
Gloucestershire beat Middlesex by 61 runs

GLOUCESTERSHIRE

Batsman	First innings		Runs	Second innings		Runs
F.J.Seabrook	c Murrell	b Haig	7		b Durston	4
A.E.Dipper	c Dales	b Haig	6	c Durston	b Haig	7
W.R.Hammond	c Hearne	b Haig	5	not	out	174
B.H.Lyon	c Durston	b Haig	4	c Hendren	b Hearne	42
H.Smith +		b Durston	3	lbw	b Hearne	2
F.G.Rogers	c Dales	b Haig	0		b Hearne	0
B.S.Bloodworth	not	out	1	run	out	9
D.C.Robinson *		b Durston	0	c Lee	b Haig	24
P.T.Mills	c Murrell	b Durston	0		b Allen	3
C.W.L.Parker		b Durston	0	c Dales	b Haig	13
E.G.Dennett		b Haig	3	not	out	5
Extras	(lb 1, nb 1)		2	(b 6, lb 1, nb 4)		11
TOTAL			31	(for 9 wkts dec)		294

MIDDLESEX

Batsman	First innings		Runs	Second innings		Runs
H.W.Lee	c Lyon	b Parker	21		b Hammond	21
H.L.Dales	c Dipper	b Hammond	7	lbw	b Mills	42
J.W.Hearne	c Rogers	b Parker	6	c Hammond	b Parker	6
E.H.Hendren	c Hammond	b Parker	5	lbw	b Parker	23
R.H.Twining	c Lyon	b Parker	1		b Mills	8
G.O.B.Allen	c Dennett	b Parker	0		c & b Parker	31
F.T.Mann *	st Smith	b Parker	0	c Lyon	b Parker	22
J.L.Guise	c Lyon	b Hammond	22	c Dennett	b Parker	0
N.E.Haig		b Mills	8	lbw	b Parker	0
H.R.Murrell +	c Hammond	b Parker	2		b Parker	22
F.J.Durston	not	out	0	not	out	3
Extras	(b 1, nb 1)		2	(b 2, lb 8, nb 2)		12
TOTAL			74			190

MIDDLESEX	O	M	R	W	O	M	R	W
Haig	12	7	11	6	33	2	95	3
Durston	11	5	18	4	16	3	61	1
Allen					9.2	1	26	1
Hearne					21	1	75	3
Lee					5	1	9	0
Murrell					4	0	17	0

GLOUCESTERSHIRE	O	M	R	W	O	M	R	W
Hammond	9	2	27	2	13	8	22	1
Parker	10.1	3	30	7	31.1	5	101	7
Mills	2	0	15	1	15	4	45	2
Dennett					8	4	10	0

FALL OF WICKETS

	G 1st	M 1st	G 2nd	M 2nd
1st	7	19	12	46
2nd	17	30	12	59
3rd	21	39	99	79
4th	24	41	102	104
5th	26	41	102	104
6th	26	41	131	136
7th	26	56	202	136
8th	26	65	205	136
9th	26	74	264	173
10th	31	74		190

Umpires: W.Phillips and W.Reeves

ESSEX

Like many other great spinners, Charlie Parker started his county career as a seam bowler. In his own mind, Parker continued for too long in a quicker style, and even when the switch took place, some of the Gloucestershire officials were still not in accord. For several years, the committeemen had told him to leave the spinning job to George Dennett, but when Dennett was still on active service in India in 1919, Parker delivered an ultimatum to the club – 'I will bowl spinners from now on and if you don't like it, I will find another county that does.'

Without anyone else to turn to, Parker won the argument, and subsequently took over 100 wickets on eleven occasions with his left-arm spin, while in 1925 during the contest against Essex at the Wagon Works ground in Gloucester, Parker returned the best ever match figures for the county. When play began on the Saturday morning, Gloucestershire put the visitors in, and in the next couple of hours, Parker took 9/44. He completely confounded the Essex men with his immaculate length, astute flight and sharp spin, on a wicket that was giving him only the very slightest assistance. The only wicket not to fall to Parker was Charlie Russell, who was run out as he and his partner got their calling wrong as they hastily tried to avoid facing the spinner.

During the afternoon session, Gloucestershire also found run-scoring quite difficult, but with Alf Dipper in dogged mood, they ended the day on 120 for 2. Heavy rain throughout Monday meant that it was not until the Tuesday morning that the home team had a chance to extend their lead. Dipper remained steadfast, and with a delightful cameo from Wally Hammond, plus an unbeaten 35

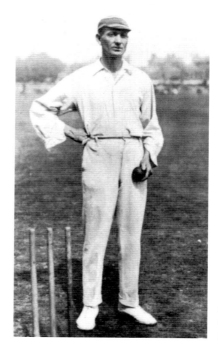

Charlie Parker – Gloucestershire's master spinner.

GLOUCESTERSHIRE v ESSEX

Played at Gloucester on 25th, 27th, 28th July 1925   Toss: Gloucestershire
Gloucestershire beat Essex by an innings and 109 runs

ESSEX

J.R.Freeman +	c Hammond	b Parker	18 (2)	lbw	b Parker	2
L.C.Eastman *	c Robinson	b Parker	16 (7)	c Hammond	b Parker	11
J.O'Connor		b Parker	18		b Parker	21
C.A.G.Russell	run	out	0	c Hammond	b Parker	0
P.A.Perrin	c Hammond	b Parker	2	c Hammond	b Parker	2
C.T.Ashton	lbw	b Parker	0		b Parker	0
J.A.Cutmore	lbw	b Parker	14 (1)		b Dennett	0
R.C.G.Joy	st Smith	b Parker	4		b Dennett	17
H.M.Morris	not	out	21	c Hammond	b Parker	5
A.B.Hipkin	c Dennett	b Parker	9		b Parker	2
M.S.Nichols		b Parker	11		not out	0
Extras	(b 1, lb 1)		2	(b 2, lb 1)		3
TOTAL			115			63

GLOUCESTERSHIRE

D.C.Robinson *	c Russell	b Hipkin	22
A.E.Dipper		b Russell	107
H.Smith +	c O'Connor	b Eastman	16
R.A.Sinfield	c Morris	b Eastman	23
W.R.Hammond	st Freeman	b Eastman	40
B.S.Bloodworth	not	out	35
R.G.W.Melsome	c Joy	b Hipkin	25
G.Wedel	not	out	5
C.W.L.Parker			
E.G.Dennett			
T.W.J.Goddard			
Extras	(b 7, lb 7)		14
TOTAL	(for 6 wkts dec)		287

GLOUCESTERSHIRE	O	M	R	W		O	M	R	W
Parker	31.3	12	44	9		17	10	12	8
Dennett	27	8	58	0		17	5	48	2
Wedel	4	1	11	0					

ESSEX	O	M	R	W
Nichols	10	4	26	0
Eastman	28	5	77	3
Hipkin	29	8	66	2
O'Connor	9	1	27	0
Ashton	12	2	43	0
Russell	15	3	32	1
Joy	2	1	2	0

FALL OF WICKETS

	E	G	E
	1st	1st	2nd
1st	25	44	0
2nd	42	85	12
3rd	50	141	12
4th	53	214	27
5th	53	222	27
6th	64	275	30
7th	70		43
8th	77		57
9th	91		59
10th	115		63

Umpires: A.E.Street and H.Chidgey

from Bernie Bloodworth, Dipper saw Gloucestershire to a lead of 172 when Douglas Robinson declared just before three o'clock.

If Gloucestershire were to win, it would need something out of the ordinary from their bowlers, but C.W.L. Parker was just the man for the job on a wicket that was starting to give generous assistance to the slow bowlers. He was virtually unplayable, taking 8/12 in 17 overs of spiteful spin, and for the second time in the match, he single-handedly dismantled the visiting batting. After Parker's earlier spat with the committee, there was more than a touch of irony that it was the veteran Dennett who took the other two wickets and prevented Parker from taking all ten in the innings.

LANCASHIRE

Those who saw it were never in doubt – neither was Neville Cardus who wrote a glowing eulogy in the *Manchester Guardian* – that Wally Hammond's unbeaten 250 against Lancashire at Old Trafford in 1925 was the finest innings the great Gloucestershire batsman ever played in Britain.

At the time, the Lancashire attack was regarded as the most potent in the country; in the minds of some observers, it was viewed as the best ever assembled by a county side. At its spearhead was the pace of Ted McDonald, who had developed a fearsome reputation opening the bowling for Australia. During his time in Test, league and county cricket, few batsmen had ever taken any liberties with the pace bowler, certainly not a callow twenty-two year old, and an Englishman to boot. But that is exactly what Wally Hammond did during a glorious third-wicket partnership of 330 in the space of four hours with Alf Dipper.

Hammond had arrived in Manchester not in the greatest of form, and as he later wrote in his autobiography *Cricket My Destiny*, he began rather shakily as he played and missed on several occasions to McDonald. 'But afterwards, I found that I could see the ball easily, and then began to go for it and sent it flying. McDonald began to shorten the ball... to flinch away from those searing leg-side bumpers would result in a nasty injury or a silly catch, so I took the only course and hit them. I recall sending one onto the pavilion roof, and after that they lost their terrors, and I could stand up to them with something like enjoyment.'

Time and again, Hammond despatched McDonald and the rest of the Lancashire side with ease, and it wasn't just Hammond who was giving the home bowlers a mauling, as at the other end, Alf

Wally Hammond

Ted McDonald

```
                    LANCASHIRE v GLOUCESTERSHIRE

Played at Manchester on 19th, 20th, 21st August 1925      Toss: Gloucestershire
Match Drawn

                            GLOUCESTERSHIRE
D.C.Robinson *    c Tyldesley  b McDonald    18    c McDonald   b Sibbles     7
A.E.Dipper        c Parkin     b Watson     144        not      out          28
R.A.Sinfield         lbw       b McDonald     0        not      out          17
W.R.Hammond          not       out          250
B.S.Bloodworth +  c Tyldesley  b Watson       1
R.Horton          c Duckworth  b McDonald     7
C.W.L.Parker      c McDonald   b Sibbles     10
G.Wedel              lbw       b Sibbles      0
J.G.W.T.Bessant                b McDonald     6
T.W.J.Goddard     c Duckworth  b McDonald     0
P.T.Mills                      b Tyldesley    5
   Extras         (b 13, lb 2)               15    (lb 1)                     1
                                            ---                            ---
   TOTAL                                     456    (for 1 wkt)             53

                            LANCASHIRE
C.Hallows         c Robinson     b Hammond   13
A.W.Pewtress         lbw         b Wedel     33
H.D.Davies        st Bloodworth  b Parker    39
F.Watson                         b Mills     93
J.Iddon              lbw         b Parker    10
J.Sharp *         c Hammond      b Mills     75
R.K.Tyldesley     c Wedel        b Parker    27
F.M.Sibbles       c Hammond      b Mills      5
C.H.Parkin           not         out          1
G.Duckworth +        lbw         b Parker     2
E.A.McDonald      c Hammond      b Parker     7
   Extras         (b 12, lb 4, w 2)          18
                                            ---
   TOTAL                                     323
```

LANCASHIRE	O	M	R	W	O	M	R	W	FALL OF WICKETS		
									G	L	G
McDonald	29	3	128	5	8	0	28	0		1st	1st	2nd
Sibbles	17	5	40	2	10	4	19	1			
Tyldesley	34.1	6	106	1					1st	20	25	7
Parkin	14	2	62	0					2nd	20	72
Watson	22	2	73	2	3	2	5	0	3rd	350	113
Iddon	7	0	32	0					4th	356	153
									5th	393	270
GLOUCESTERSHIRE									6th	418	297
Goddard	5	1	18	0					7th	418	312
Hammond	14	3	36	1					8th	435	313
Parker	51.1	16	120	5					9th	435	315
Wedel	21	8	35	1					10th	456	323
Horton	14	4	21	0							
Mills	27	11	46	3							
Sinfield	13	3	29	0							

```
Umpires: W.A.Buswell and W.Reeves
```

Dipper, the wise old professional, was far from being a sleeping partner, striking a fine 144. It came at a tempo far quicker than normal as he benefited from Hammond's youthful assault, and as the bowlers wilted, Dipper unleashed some savage blows of his own.

When Gloucestershire's innings ended, Hammond departed to a richly deserved standing ovation from the Mancunian supporters, many of whom had never before seen such a brilliant attack on the county's much-vaunted bowlers. The watching journalists were equally fulsome in their praise, while the headline writers gave due prominence to Hammond's remarkable feat and ensured that his batting exploits could hardly be ignored even by the most casual of readers.

SURREY

15, 16, 17 August 1928 at Cheltenham

There has perhaps never been a Cheltenham Festival quite like it – a week of cricket where one man with both bat and ball overshadowed the feats of every other player who took the field in front of the famous college buildings. The year was 1928, and the player in question was Wally Hammond, now fully restored after the debilitating illness contracted on England's tour in 1925/26 to the West Indies that had robbed him of a summer's cricket on his return from the Caribbean, and but for urgent medical treatment, had nearly taken his life.

These dark hours, spent convalescing in a nursing home, were light years away as Hammond, under clear blue skies, began the Festival by scoring 139 and 143 against Surrey, off-driving the bowlers with awesome power and timing, and effortlessly sending the ball skimming down the slope towards the Gothic chapel. For their part, Surrey had the great Jack Hobbs, but his scores of 96 and 2 almost pale into insignificance alongside Hammond's pair of masterly centuries that thrilled the Cheltenham crowd, and so exquisite was his placement that the Surrey fielders simply gave up trying to defend the boundary in front of the chapel.

But Hammond's role in this classic match was not just restricted to one with the bat. He opened the bowling in Surrey's first innings, and took ten catches in the slips – a county record – including five in succession from Charlie Parker's left-arm spin as Surrey attempted to score 357 on the final day. After Hammond's wondrous batting, it was a task that was too great for Surrey, especially after Hobbs had departed in Parker's opening burst.

Soon afterwards, Reg Sinfield dismissed Andy Sandham, and despite a defiant half-century from Andy Ducat, Parker steadily worked his way, with the help of Wally Hammond at slip, through the rest of the Surrey batting, as Gloucestershire began the Festival with a comprehensive 189-run victory.

The scorecard for the Gloucestershire match against Surrey at Cheltenham in 1928.

GLOUCESTERSHIRE v SURREY

Played at Cheltenham College on 15th, 16th, 17th August 1928   Toss: Gloucestershire
Gloucestershire beat Surrey by 189 runs

GLOUCESTERSHIRE

A.E.Dipper	c & b Garland-Wells	7			c & b Peach	41
R.A.Sinfield	b Peach	0			lbw	b Shepherd	22
W.R.Hammond	c Shepherd	b Peach	139		c Gregory	b Fenley	143
B.H.Lyon *	c & b Fender	6			c Hobbs	b Shepherd	27
F.J.Seabrook	c Gregory	b Fender	0			
W.L.Neale	c Ducat	b Garland-Wells	10			b Fender	5
H.Smith +	c Fender	b Shepherd	56	(5)		b Shepherd	0
C.J.Barnett	c Garland-Wells	b Peach	0	(7)	c Ducat	b Fenley	45
M.A.Green	c Sandham	b Fenley	37	(8)	not	out	21
C.W.L.Parker	c Brooks	b Fender	19	(9)	c Shepherd	b Fenley	11
P.T.Mills	not	out	7	(10)		b Shepherd	2
Extras	(b 12, lb 10, nb 1)	23		(b 2)	2
		---			---
TOTAL		**304**		**(for 9 wkts dec)**	**319**

SURREY

J.B.Hobbs	c Seabrook	b Hammond	96	c Smith	b Parker	2
A.Sandham	c Smith	b Sinfield	0	c Hammond	b Sinfield	10
A.Ducat	c Dipper	b Parker	6	c Hammond	b Parker	55
T.F.Shepherd	c Barnett	b Parker	52	c Hammond	b Parker	17
T.H.Barling	c Hammond	b Parker	4	c Hammond	b Parker	2
R.J.Gregory	c Hammond	b Parker	7	c Hammond	b Parker	3
P.G.H.Fender *	c Hammond	b Sinfield	55	c Hammond	b Parker	20
H.M.Garland-Wells	c Hammond	b Parker	6	st Smith	b Sinfield	49
H.A.Peach		b Mills	5	c Smith	b Parker	1
E.W.J.Brooks +	lbw	b Parker	2	run	out	0
S.Fenley	not	out	0	not	out	0
Extras	(b 27, lb 7)	34	(b 1, lb 7)	8
		---			---
TOTAL		**267**			**167**

SURREY	O	M	R	W	O	M	R	W		FALL OF WICKETS			
Fender	24.3	10	57	3	25	6	55	1			G	S	G	S
Peach	27	6	68	3	26	9	71	1			1st	1st	2nd	2nd
Fenley	12	2	44	1	18	2	83	3		1st	2	8	55	3
Shepherd	15	4	43	1	32.4	5	74	4		2nd	70	40	79	13
Garland-Wells	22	5	65	2	14	3	34	0		3rd	95	120	131	55
Gregory	2	0	4	0						4th	95	136	156	57
										5th	112	174	171	69
GLOUCESTERSHIRE										6th	201	224	274	107
Hammond	22	3	71	1						7th	205	233	287	122
Sinfield	9	4	10	2	27	9	59	2		8th	256	238	298	140
Parker	38.4	6	117	6	32	10	80	7		9th	280	265	319	158
Mills	24	11	35	1	6	0	20	0		10th	304	267		167

Umpires: W.Bestwick and J.King

WORCESTERSHIRE

18, 20 August 1928 at Cheltenham

The second game of the 1928 Cheltenham Festival was a local derby against Worcestershire, and hordes of their supporters travelled to the Regency town in anticipation of seeing the great Wally Hammond in all his pomp and majesty. They were not disappointed, but it was as a bowler that Hammond made an impact on this match claiming 15 wickets in the match as Worcestershire were completely outplayed.

Worcestershire batted first but Hammond found the overcast conditions and slightly damp wicket just to his liking, and his cutters exposed the weaknesses of some over-cautious batsmen. Forsaking his usual style for something slightly slower, Hammond returned career-best figures of 9/23, and he proved himself almost unplayable on a wicket whose surface had been dampened by the morning dew. He also had a hand in the other wicket to fall, as Bernard Quaife jabbed a catch into Hammond's hands in the gully off Parker's left-arm spin.

Worcestershire mustered just 35, and as the heavy dew evaporated under the afternoon sun, it only took a few overs for Gloucestershire to take the lead. Dipper and Sinfield took their opening stand to 116, before Hammond and his captain Bev Lyon enjoyed a run spree of 108 as Gloucestershire finished the opening day 246 runs ahead with five wickets in hand.

After a day of rest on the Sunday, runs continued to flow for Gloucestershire and shortly after Billy Neale had reached fifty, Bev Lyon eventually declared with his side having a handsome lead of 335. Worcestershire went in again, and in slightly less overcast conditions, they found batting slightly easier, but this time Hammond soon reverted to off-spin, and with

Charlie Parker

Wally Hammond

```
                    GLOUCESTERSHIRE v WORCESTERSHIRE

Played at Cheltenham College on 18th, 20th August 1928      Toss: Worcestershire
Gloucestershire beat Worcestershire by an innings and 168 runs

                               WORCESTERSHIRE
J.B.Higgins *                  b Hammond      2    c Lyon        b Parker    35
L.Wright           st Smith    b Hammond      8                  b Parker     1
B.W.Quaife         c Hammond   b Parker       2    c Seabrook    b Hammond   19
W.V.Fox            c Lyon      b Hammond      1    c Lyon        b Hammond    1
H.H.I.H.Gibbons    c Stephens  b Hammond      4    c Lyon        b Parker     9
C.F.Root           c Seabrook  b Hammond      0       lbw        b Hammond    1
C.V.Tarbox                     b Hammond      6    c Barnett     b Hammond   29
J.W.King              not         out         0    c Seabrook    b Hammond    4
J.J.Bowles         c Lyon      b Hammond      4    hit wicket  b Parker      20
D.V.Hill           c Parker    b Hammond      0    st Smith      b Hammond   17
F.T.Summers +                  b Hammond      0       not          out        0
     Extras        (b 5, lb 3)                8    (b 21, lb 10)             31
                                            ---                             ---
     TOTAL                                    35                            167

                               GLOUCESTERSHIRE
A.E.Dipper         c Quaife    b Wright      77
R.A.Sinfield       c Hill      b Wright      30
W.R.Hammond        c Summers   b Wright      80
B.H.Lyon *                     b Tarbox      38
F.J.Seabrook                   b Hill        29
H.Smith +             lbw      b Hill         6
W.L.Neale             not         out        51
C.J.Barnett           not         out        34
E.J.Stephens
C.W.L.Parker
P.T.Mills
     Extras        (b 15, lb 9, nb 1)        25
                                            ---
     TOTAL                   (for 6 wkts dec) 370
```

GLOUCESTERSHIRE	O	M	R	W	O	M	R	W	FALL OF WICKETS			
										W	G	W
Hammond	10.2	2	23	9	33.3	5	105	6		1st	1st	2nd
Sinfield	2	1	3	0					1st	8	116	6
Parker	8	7	1	1	33	22	31	4	2nd	15	117	67
									3rd	19	225	69
WORCESTERSHIRE									4th	19	266	73
Root	36	10	82	0					5th	19	272	78
Hill	20	1	71	2					6th	24	290	116
Bowles	17	3	49	0					7th	31		117
Tarbox	30	5	88	1					8th	35		137
Wright	20	4	55	3					9th	35		167
									10th	35		167

```
Umpires: W.Bestwick and J.King
```

immaculate control, he tied down the visitors, and was no less effective than Charlie Parker at the other end.

Despite some stubborn resistance, wickets continued to fall at regular intervals against the combined wiles of Parker and Hammond, with the latter adding a further six wickets to his tally. The game finished on the second evening as Gloucestershire recorded an innings victory with Hammond ending up with a match haul of 15 wickets to prove that his prowess as a cricketer did not only lie in his wonderful batting.

AUSTRALIANS

23, 25, 26 August 1930 at Bristol

'The most exciting match of all' – that is how Wally Hammond, a man who rarely elaborated in public on his emotions, described the match between Gloucestershire and the 1930 Australians. 'There were no sensations, no huge totals – just a pitiless struggle between ball and bat in which everyone on that green field played as if for his life, while those who looked on were so tense that they could hardly bear to clap or shout.'

It always looked like being a good contest, given the fact that the Gloucestershire side boasted Wally Hammond, England's premier batsman, and spinners Tom Goddard and Charlie Parker, both of whom were at the top of their form, taking 293 wickets between them during the summer. And just for good measure, there was Bev Lyon's shrewd captaincy, making it a contest that was never going to a pushover for the tourists.

The Australians arrived in Bristol in good heart, having won the Ashes at The Oval. For this reason the start time was put back to two o'clock, but as it turned out, rain prevented any play until four o'clock. After winning the toss, Vic Richardson inserted the home batsmen, with the damp, heavy atmosphere making it ideal for bowling. Clarrie Grimmett's leg-breaks, always metronomic in their accuracy, were soon curving in menacingly to the batsmen in the overcast conditions, but it was Hornibrook's left-arm spin that made the greatest impact, and despite an hour's resistance

The Nevil Road ground – the scene of the 'most exciting match of all'.

Clarrie Cormmere

from Wally Hammond, Gloucestershire's first innings ended after only two-and-a-quarter-hour's play.

On the Monday morning, the Australians also found batting difficult on the damp wicket, losing their first seven wickets for just 64 runs. Don Bradman batted for an hour and three-quarters to make a disciplined 42, but in truth, he was never at ease against the Gloucestershire spinners, and it was largely the result of an assertive half-century from Bill Ponsford that the tourists secured a lead of 85.

When Gloucestershire batted for a second time, much depended on Hammond if they were going to secure a challenging position, something that the tourists were only too well aware of, and as the master batsman later recalled, 'not even in many Test innings have I been flattered with such unflinching attention, or so many and such wicked traps. Eleven men willed me not to run – or if I ran to run myself out.'

With Dipper dropping anchor at one end, Hammond skilfully farmed Grimmett at the other, scoring an accomplished 89 and drawing on all of his experience at Test level against the fiery Australian attack. Harry Smith also lent valuable support, and when the last wicket fell, it meant that Australia needed 118 to win. On paper it was a very small target, especially given the fact that in the Test series the Aussies had amassed totals of 729, 695 and 566 against the cream of English bowling. But against Goddard, Parker and the rest of the Gloucestershire attack with their tails up, and egged on by a capacity crowd, the tourists knew they were going to be made to fight for every run.

As the Gloucestershire side took to the field, a huge roar echoed around the ground, and if that wasn't enough to lift the players, Lyon called his troops around and said 'Take it steady boys – you can do it on your own on this wicket.' But it soon looked as if the situation was getting to Parker who bowled erratically in the opening forty minutes, as Jackson and McCabe added 59 for the first wicket. Parker gradually found his length and started to regularly hit a worn spot, and by the time lunch was taken, the tourists had quickly slipped to 67 for 3 as batting became increasingly difficult.

Even so, the visitors were still in the driving seat, but soon after the game resumed, it took a dramatic turn as Parker trapped Kippax leg before, and then without another run being added, Reg Sinfield ran out Ponsford. Australian spirits were lifted by the presence of the great Don Bradman, but only 8 more runs had been added when Parker bowled Bradman with a beauty. A'Beckett soon followed, and although Lyon dropped Grimmett, tigerish fielding supported by immaculate bowling kept the tourists well in check.

Grimmett and Hurwood added 22 for the eighth wicket before the latter was trapped lbw to leave the tourists just 10 runs away from their target. The tension started to mount as both Parker and Goddard had appeals turned down, and a further 7 runs were eked out before Parker had Grimmett caught after defying the Gloucester attack for over an hour.

Australians

Hornibrook was then joined by Walker and a couple of scrambled singles brought the scores level, and the tension became unbearable as the tail-enders frequently played and missed as they lunged forward in the hope of laying bat on ball. Goddard had another appeal turned down against Hornibrook, whilst Parker beat Walker with a beauty, but the ball then brushed off the stumps without dislodging the bails. In an attempt to break the impasse, Hornibrook danced down the wicket in an attempt to chip the ball over the gaggle of in-fielders, but rather than hitting the winning runs, he miscued the ball back towards the non-striker, and had to quickly scurry back into his crease.

Then Goddard struck Hornibrook on the pads – 'How waz 'ee then' came the booming baritone appeal. After due consideration, umpire Buswell slowly raised his finger to a deafening roar from the 17,000 spectators, who seconds later surged onto the ground to congratulate their heroes who had become the first county team to tie a game against the Australians.

As Hammond later wrote, 'it was as if the walls of a dam had burst. We were inundated – players were slung up onto shoulders with as little care as sacks of wheat – Tom Goddard's arms and legs jerked like semaphores as he tried to keep his balance. A continuous deafening shouting stupefied the senses, and a thousand hands beat our backs and wrung our arms almost from their sockets.'

The Glorious Glosters eventually made their way to Temple Meads railway station to catch the train to Swansea for the game the following day against Glamorgan, but even at Brunel's grand masterpiece, the approach to the station, the booking hall and even the platforms themselves were full of a cheering throng who all wanted to make their own contribution to the celebrations. On their journey to West Wales, the amateurs and professionals celebrated together by swigging from bottles

Tom Goddard – the man who took the final wicket in the tied match with the 1930 Australians.

```
                        GLOUCESTERSHIRE v AUSTRALIANS

Played at Bristol on 23rd, 25th, 26th August 1930          Toss: Australians
Match Tied

                              GLOUCESTERSHIRE
R.A.Sinfield     c Walker     b Hurwood      1 ( 2) c a'Beckett  b Hornibrook  16
A.E.Dipper       c Richardson b Hurwood      1 ( 1) c a'Beckett  b McCabe      26
W.R.Hammond      c a'Beckett  b Hornibrook  17                   b Hornibrook  89
B.H.Lyon *                    b Hurwood      5                   b McCabe       8
H.Smith +        c Richardson b Hornibrook  16                   b Hornibrook  23
C.C.R.Dacre      c a'Beckett  b Grimmett     4        c McCabe    b Grimmett    17
F.J.Seabrook              c & b Grimmett    19        lbw         b Hornibrook   2
W.L.Neale        c Walker     b Hornibrook   2 ( 9)               b Hornibrook   0
C.J.Barnett                   b Grimmett     2 ( 8) c Walker      b Grimmett     6
C.W.L.Parker            not         out      0                    not    out    3
T.W.J.Goddard    c Kippax     b Hornibrook   3                    run    out    0
   Extras        (lb 2)                      2        (b 6, lb 6)               12
                                            ---                                ---
   TOTAL                                     72                                202

                                AUSTRALIANS
W.H.Ponsford                  b Sinfield    51 ( 6)    run         out          0
A.Jackson                     b Goddard      8 ( 1)    lbw         b Goddard    25
D.G.Bradman      c Seabrook   b Parker      42 ( 4)                b Parker     14
A.F.Kippax           lbw      b Sinfield     3 ( 5)    lbw         b Parker      0
S.J.McCabe       c Smith      b Parker       5 ( 2)                b Parker     34
V.Y.Richardson *     lbw      b Goddard     12 ( 3) st Smith       b Parker      3
E.L.a'Beckett    c Sinfield   b Goddard      1        c Lyon       b Parker      2
A.Hurwood                     b Goddard      0 ( 9)    lbw         b Parker     14
C.V.Grimmett         not          out        7 ( 8) c Seabrook     b Parker     12
P.M.Hornibrook                b Goddard      9        lbw          b Goddard     4
C.W.Walker +     c Seabrook   b Parker       7        not          out          0
   Extras        (b 5, lb 7)                12        (b 2, lb 7)                9
                                           ---                                ---
   TOTAL                                    157                                117

AUSTRALIANS    O    M    R    W      O    M    R    W     FALL OF WICKETS
a'Beckett      8    4    9    0      9    4   16    0              G    A    G    A
Hurwood       11    5   13    3     11    4   29    0            1st  1st  2nd  2nd
Grimmett      18    3   28    3   28.2    4   83    2      1st     2   42   21   59
Hornibrook  14.3    6   20    4     25    5   49    5      2nd     3   78  101   63
McCabe                             10    3   13    2      3rd    17   88  113   67
                                                          4th    30   96  166   73
GLOUCESTERSHIRE                                           5th    35  129  187   73
Sinfield      14    5   18    2                           6th    53  131  192   81
Barnett        4    3    3    0                           7th    67  131  199   86
Goddard       26    7   52    5   34.1   10   54    2     8th    69  131  199  108
Parker      30.5    9   72    3     35   14   54    7     9th    69  140  201  115
                                                         10th    72  157  202  117

Umpires: W.A.Buswell and W.Huddleston
```

of scotch in their reserved compartments on the GWR express, with each member of the team radiant in the knowledge that had collectively achieved something that the national side had failed to do.

The next day, while changing in the pavilion at St Helen's, many of the players were still smarting from the incessant backslapping. Several had huge black and blue marks on their backs, but the sweet taste of success, fuelled by more than just the odd glass of champagne, helped to take away whatever pain was there. The bruises may have quickly healed, but the happy memories of that wonderful, heart-stopping afternoon at Bristol remained with Bev Lyon and his team forever. As Lyon later commented 'any captain can win or lose a game against the Australians, but there are bloody few who can tie one!'

WEST INDIANS

The Australians were not the first touring team to struggle in matches at Bristol. In 1900 the West Indians were beaten by an innings in a match, not recognised as first-class, that saw no less than three Gloucestershire batsmen – Harry Wrathall, Charles Townsend, and Gilbert Jessop – score centuries as the home team made 619 against the Caribbean bowlers.

Thirty-three years later, the West Country side recorded another victory with Hammond making a sublime double hundred against the West Indian bowlers, and with over 500 runs in the bank, they forced the tourists to follow-on after accurate spin bowling from Tom Goddard and Billy Neale, ably supported by the medium pace of Reg Sinfield.

After the Bodyline controversy during the winter, Hammond batted like a dream following his return to British shores in the spring of 1933 and he enjoyed a highly prolific summer. Hammond came into this match against the Caribbean tourists on the back of a double century against Derbyshire at the Cheltenham Festival, and he continued his fine form as Gloucestershire took first use of the wicket, making 264 in six hours and ten minutes, during which he struck twenty-two crisp boundaries.

From a personal point of view, Hammond's double hundred against the tourists must have given him especial pleasure given the near fatal illness which he had contracted on the Caribbean tour in 1925/26. When he reached the 200 mark, early on the second morning, many could have forgiven him for having a smile that was broader than usual.

Above left: Charles Barnett – Gloucestershire's prolific opening batsman.

Above right: Grahame Parker – the Cambridge University Blue who later became the Gloucestershire secretary.

```
                    GLOUCESTERSHIRE v WEST INDIANS

Played at Bristol on 19th, 21st 22nd August 1933        Toss: Gloucestershire
Gloucestershire beat West Indians by 7 wickets

                              GLOUCESTERSHIRE
B.O.Allen              run        out       11 ( 3)  c Grant      b Achong    19
C.J.Barnett      c Roach       b Achong     60          c Merry   b Achong    27
W.R.Hammond      c Da Costa    b Achong    264 ( 4)      not       out        18
B.H.Lyon *       c Achong      b Griffith   69
C.C.R.Dacre      c Achong      b Griffith    7
F.J.Seabrook     c Christiani  b Griffith   44 ( 5)      not       out         5
R.A.Sinfield     c Hoad        b Sealy      46
G.W.Parker                     b Griffith   13 ( 1)  c Christiani b Griffith   0
W.L.Neale                      b Merry      23
P.I.van der Gucht +    not        out        3
T.W.J.Goddard    c Valentine   b Achong     13
        Extras  (b 5, lb 9, w 2, nb 1)      17       (lb 3, w 1)              4
                                           ---                              ---
        TOTAL                              570       (for 3 wkts)            73

                               WEST INDIANS
I.Barrow                       b Parker     15                  b Neale      14
E.L.G.Hoad                     b Neale      37                  b Neale      35
C.A.Roach                      b Neale      43       c Dacre    b Sinfield   22
G.C.Grant *                    b Sinfield   46                  b Sinfield  109
O.C.Da Costa     c Lyon        b Neale      20       c Seabrook b Sinfield   14
B.J.Sealy             lbw      b Goddard    87       c Dacre    b Neale      42
C.A.Merry             lbw      b Sinfield    1       c Parker   b Sinfield   26
C.M.Christiani + c Hammond     b Sinfield    8          lbw     b Sinfield   40
V.A.Valentine         not        out         4       c   sub    b Sinfield   41
E.E.Achong                     b Goddard     5       c   sub    b Sinfield    4
H.C.Griffith     c Parker      b Sinfield    1          not       out        9
        Extras  (lb 3, nb 1)                 4       (b 4, lb 10, w 1)       15
                                           ---                             ---
        TOTAL                              271                             371


WEST INDIANS      O    M    R   W     O    M    R   W      FALL OF WICKETS
Griffith         34    5  129   4     4    0   10   1        G    W    W    G
Valentine        36    0  150   0     3    1    6   0           1st  1st  2nd  2nd
Sealy            16    1   82   1     3    0   12   0    1st   61   44   25    0
Achong         34.4    3  115   1   6.2    0   32   2    2nd   82   78   68   31
Grant             1    0    6   0                       3rd  225  103   88   67
Merry            21    1   71   1     3    0    9   0    4th  234  143  133
                                                       5th  322  230  215
GLOUCESTERSHIRE                                        6th  434  234  266
Lyon             14    1   26   0                       7th  469  258  282
Barnett           5    0   10   0     6    1   17   0    8th  553  260  348
Parker           17    4   48   1    18    2   45   0    9th  555  270  360
Neale            17    0   91   3    28    4  101   3   10th  570  271  371
Sinfield       18.4    6   54   4  39.1    4  149   7
Goddard          10    0   38   2
Hammond                               6    1   22   0
Dacre                                 5    0   22   0

Umpires: J.Humphries and E.J.Smith
```

By the end of the second day, the West Indians had been dismissed for 271, so Bev Lyon had no hesitation in imposing the follow-on. His bowlers, who included Grahame Parker, once again posed problems for the tourists with Sinfield's clever cutters claiming seven victims and more than making up for the absence of Goddard. George Grant, the captain of the touring team, made a valiant attempt to save the game, but he was eventually bowled by Sinfield. Needing to score 73 in just an hour and a quarter, Gloucestershire reached their target with 10 overs to spare.

South Africans

All sportsmen need a little bit of luck at times, although I think few can claim that their bit of good fortune was linked to an insect. But that is exactly what happened in 1935 as Gloucestershire gained another Test scalp in the form of the touring South Africans, thanks to a remarkable bowling display by Reg Sinfield.

As Sinfield later recalled 'before lunch I spotted a ladybird on my shirt so I told the skipper I thought it might be my lucky day, and he put me on to bowl'. He subsequently took two wickets before lunch, and then after sitting in the pavilion during the interval and staring, with an air of expectancy and impatience, out at the wicket, he took three further wickets to wrap up a remarkable victory for the West Country side. His feats were marked afterwards by speeches by the Mayor of Cheltenham and various players, all accompanied by rapturous applause from the ecstatic crowd. What the ladybird got is not recorded!

The Springboks had hitherto been carrying all before them, and at Lord's they had beaten England by the comprehensive margin of 157 runs. In contrast, the West Country side had lost their previous seven matches and were struggling for consistency with either bat or ball. It had proved to be a rather difficult first year in charge of the team for Dallas Page, the twenty-four-year-old batsman who had taken over at the end of the previous summer from Bev Lyon.

Educated at Cheltenham College and Sandhurst, Page must have been reassured to return to his old school ground after a rather difficult start to his captaincy. There was a smile on his face when he returned to the pavilion after winning the toss. The beam was even broader as Reg Sinfield, the determined and warm-hearted opener, made a careful century.

But not everyone was smiling in the Gloucester camp – Hammond had returned to the pavilion in a furious mood after being bowled by a googly from Balaskas. Indignantly he vowed revenge, and when Gloucestershire batted again, 10 runs in arrears, Hammond compiled a masterly century with none of the Springbok bowlers being able to contain him.

Tom Goddard

Reg Sinfield

```
                      GLOUCESTERSHIRE v SOUTH AFRICANS

Played at Cheltenham College on 10th, 12th, 13th August 1935    Toss: Gloucestershire
Gloucestershire beat South Africans by 87 runs

                              GLOUCESTERSHIRE
R.A.Sinfield     c Rowan       b Tomlinson  102             b Vincent      29
E.J.Stephens     c Mitchell    b Crisp        5  ( 8) c Nourse b Balaskas  17
W.R.Hammond                     b Balaskas    38         c Crisp b Vincent 123
B.H.Lyon         c Dalton      b Balaskas     21             b Crisp       27
F.J.Seabrook                    b Vincent      3  ( 6)       lbw b Balaskas  3
W.L.Neale                       b Balaskas    61  ( 5) st Cameron b Balaskas 24
C.J.Barnett         lbw         b Crisp       24  ( 2)       lbw b Vincent  46
D.A.C.Page *     st Cameron     b Mitchell     1  ( 7)       lbw b Vincent  11
C.W.L.Parker           c & b Balaskas         14         c Nourse b Vincent  9
T.W.J.Goddard                   b Crisp        0         c Tomlinson b Vincent 0
H.Smith +            not            out         3             not     out    0
   Extras         (b 2, lb 3, nb 2)            7         (b 8, lb 1)         9
                                              ---                          ---
   TOTAL                                      279                          298

                              SOUTH AFRICANS
B.Mitchell                      b Hammond     10         c Page  b Parker   25
E.A.B.Rowan                     b Goddard     31  ( 3) c Barnett b Sinfield 39
K.G.Viljoen      c Lyon        b Sinfield    122  ( 5)       lbw b Hammond  33
A.D.Nourse          lbw         b Parker       9             b Goddard      16
I.J.Siedle             c & b Goddard           0  ( 2)       lbw b Sinfield 44
H.B.Cameron *+   st Smith       b Parker      39             lbw b Sinfield  0
E.L.Dalton       c Lyon         b Hammond     48             b Goddard      22
X.C.Balaskas                    b Sinfield     7             lbw b Sinfield  0
C.L.Vincent            c & b Sinfield          0  (10) c Smith b Sinfield   17
R.J.Crisp        c Page         b Hammond      5  ( 9) c Barnett b Goddard   0
D.S.Tomlinson       not            out         2             not     out     1
   Extras         (b 4, lb 12)                16         (lb 3, nb 1)        4
                                              ---                          ---
   TOTAL                                      289                          201
```

SOUTH AFRICANS	O	M	R	W	O	M	R	W	FALL OF WICKETS				
Crisp	17	1	50	3	13	0	49	1		G	S	G	S
Viljoen	3	2	10	0	2	0	3	0		1st	1st	2nd	2nd
Balaskas	30	0	101	4	25.4	0	124	3	1st	11	43	54	53
Vincent	15	3	42	1	27	4	90	6	2nd	68	53	109	75
Tomlinson	8	0	43	1					3rd	114	100	189	107
Mitchell	8	0	26	1					4th	124	107	253	150
Dalton					5	0	23	0	5th	226	182	259	150
									6th	243	258	263	170
GLOUCESTERSHIRE									7th	246	279	272	182
Barnett	6	0	27	0	5	2	9	0	8th	269	279	292	182
Hammond	15	1	47	3	11	2	23	1	9th	269	286	295	187
Goddard	29	8	70	2	20	7	65	3	10th	279	289	298	201
Parker	24	3	88	2	30	5	69	1					
Sinfield	9.5	1	41	3	15.3	5	31	5					

Umpires: W.R.Parry and W.Bestwick

Through his efforts, Gloucestershire gained a lead of 289, but rain swept down from the Cotswolds to prevent the Springboks from starting their innings until the following day. At lunch, they had moved on serenely to within 150 of their target, but the introduction of Sinfield's medium pace changed everything. In the space of an hour they collapsed from 150 for 3 to 201 all out. Sinfield took 5/31 with his subtle changes of flight and pace, plus a clever arm ball that confounded their batsmen. As the euphoric crowd went into Cheltenham's watering holes, Sinfield became the toast of the town, and all thanks to a lucky ladybird!

INDIANS

8, 10, 11 August 1936 at Cheltenham

To many people, especially those who passionately followed Gloucestershire cricket during the 1920s and 1930s, it was a complete mystery why Reg Sinfield only played once in Test cricket for England. In 1934 he had become the first Gloucestershire professional to perform the double of 1,000 runs and 100 wickets in a season for the county, and time and again his steady batting or incisive bowling helped to secure outstanding victories for his county.

An example came in 1936 at the Cheltenham Festival, with Sinfield and Wally Hammond playing major roles in Gloucestershire's victory over the Indian tourists. The two were close friends, with Sinfield getting on much better with Hammond than many of his colleagues. A whimsical relationship developed between the warm-hearted all-rounder and the rather complex and private master batsman, so much so that when Hammond became the county's captain, he would take his lieutenant out to the middle to look at the wicket before the toss and to bounce ideas off his trusted ally prior to any decisions being made.

On this particular occasion, it was 'Puggy' Page who was at the helm, and his decision to keep Sinfield going in mid-afternoon with his canny medium-paced bowling resulted in the jaunty all-rounder finishing off the Indian first innings, taking their last four wickets, without conceding a run. Then it was over to Hammond, who hit a majestic 81 on a typical Cheltenham wicket where only one other batsman passed fifty, and the bowlers generally held the upper hand. Whereas the wiles of the Indian bowlers proved too much for many of the other Gloucestershire batsmen, they held no terrors for either Hammond, or his trusted ally Sinfield, who struck a typically dogged 45 as the home team gained a first-innings lead of 159.

The Indians' second innings then began where the first one had ended with Sinfield posing problems with his crafty medium pace, and by the close of the second day, India had slipped to 123 for 6, and an innings defeat loomed. But a ninth wicket partnership of exactly 100 between Baqa Jilani and Amir Elahi avoided this, until Sinfield – who else? – ended their resistance,

The Gloucestershire team in 1936. From left to right, standing: B.S. Bloodworth, C.J. Barnett, R. Sinfield, W.L. Neale, V.C. Hopkins, R. Haynes. Sitting: W.R. Hammond, T.W. Goddard, B.O. Allen, E.J. Stephens, C.C. Dacre.

```
                        GLOUCESTERSHIRE v INDIANS

Played at Cheltenham College on 8th, 10th, 11th August 1936    Toss: Indians
Gloucestershire beat Indians by 8 wickets

                                INDIANS
V.M.Merchant              b Barnett      8   c Hammond   b Cranfield   37
Dilawar Hussain +    lbw  b Hammond      3   c Page      b Sinfield    24
Sir V.A.Vizianagram *     b Cranfield   39       lbw    b Sinfield     6
C.K.Nayudu           lbw  b Tyler       17   c Tyler     b Emmett      40
S.Wazir Ali               b Tyler       31   st Wilson   b Sinfield    27
S.Mushtaq Ali    c Wilson b Barnett     23   c Tyler     b Cranfield    2
C.Ramaswami          lbw  b Sinfield    22               b Cranfield    4
M. Baqa Jilani   c Wilson b Sinfield     1               b Sinfield    59
S.N.Banerjee              b Sinfield     0               b Cranfield    6
Amir Elahi           not  out            2   c Page      b Sinfield    45
Mohammad Nissar  c Page   b Sinfield     0      not      out            1
    Extras      (b 4, lb 3, nb 1)        8   (b 2, lb 7)                9
                                       ---                            ---
    TOTAL                               154                            260

                            GLOUCESTERSHIRE
C.J.Barnett               b Nissar      17               b Jilani      16
D.N.Moore            lbw  b Jilani      35      not      out           44
G.M.Emmett                b Jilani      26      lbw      b Jilani       0
W.R.Hammond               b Nayudu      81      not      out           35
J.F.Crapp                 b Nissar       9
R.A.Sinfield  c Ramaswami b Banerjee    45
D.A.C.Page *  c Wazir Ali b Jilani      20
E.J.Stephens    c Jilani  b Merchant    17
A.E.Wilson +         lbw  b Nayudu      17
L.M.Cranfield        not  out            8
C.Tyler                   b Nissar      22
    Extras       (b 8, lb 8)            16   (b 8, lb 1)                9
                                       ---                            ---
    TOTAL                               313   (for 2 wkts)            104

GLOUCESTERSHIRE   O    M   R   W      O    M   R   W    FALL OF WICKETS
Hammond           7    1  14   1     18    4  45   0        I    G   I    G
Barnett          18    8  23   2      9    3  14   0       1st  1st 2nd 2nd
Cranfield        21    7  44   1     19    4  43   4    1st   9   18  41   29
Tyler            12    2  27   2     10    4  32   0    2nd  15   76  60   29
Sinfield       27.2  13  38   4   35.5   11  79   5    3rd  48  107 104
Emmett                               12    3  38   1    4th  80  126 113
                                                       5th 128  207 115
INDIANS                                                6th 147  235 123
Nissar         16.2   4  49   3      5    0  15   0    7th 151  244 148
Banerjee         11   1  29   1      4    2  10   0    8th 151  283 155
Nayudu           29   8  86   2      6    0  18   0    9th 152  287 255
Merchant          9   2  35   1                       10th 154  313 260
Elahi             8   1  32   0      3    1   9   0
Jilani           21   3  46   3      9    0  32   2
Mushtaq Ali       6   1  20   0
Wazir Ali                            1    0   6   0
Vizianagram                        0.4    0   5   0

Umpires: J.Hardstaff and J.A.Newman
```

dismissing both men, before the Gloucestershire batsmen coasted to an eight-wicket victory.

Sinfield's match haul of nine wickets was a worthy reward for one of the most popular faces in the West Country side, and a man who always played tenaciously for his team. Sinfield never gave less than 100 per cent on the field for Gloucestershire CCC, yet he always kept a genial smile on his face off the field: as one fellow county cricketer once remarked, 'Gloucestershire were not exactly the height of conviviality at times, but dear old Reg Sinfield was invariably the exception. He always had a cheery greeting – even if he was planning to tweak you out!'

NOTTINGHAMSHIRE

29, 31 August, 1 September 1936 at Gloucester

On 1 September 1936 Gloucestershire ended their season with a morale-boosting innings victory over Nottinghamshire at the Wagon Works ground. It was a game that saw Wally Hammond record a marvellous triple hundred, and Tom Goddard, on his home town ground, take sizeable proceeds for his benefit. It seemed a grand way to finish the summer. But triumph quickly turned into tragedy as within hours of this classic match finishing, Dallas Page, the Gloucestershire captain, was killed in a car crash.

On his homeward journey to Cirencester, Page's sports car collided with a motorcyclist before ploughing into a Cotswold stone wall. At first, his injuries did not appear to be too severe, and after climbing out of the wreckage, Page went to Cirencester Hospital for a check-up. But it soon transpired that the Gloucestershire captain had suffered major internal injuries and he died during the early hours.

His death cast a sombre spectre over a game that had seen all that was best about Gloucestershire cricket in the 1930s – wonderful batting from Hammond, plus accurate bowling from the Gloucestershire spinners: in this particular case, Goddard and Monty Cranfield, on a wicket that was almost tailor made for them.

The visitors had batted first, but by tea on the first day, they had been dismissed for exactly 200, and with the wicket likely to help the bowlers throughout, Goddard was rather perturbed about the prospect of the match finishing early, and losing out on gate money. He summoned the Wagon Works groundsman, Arthur Paish, to the pavilion, and a frank discussion took place between the laconic off-spinner, and the county's former left-arm bowler. 'I relied on you, Arthur' said Goddard, 'and here it is, bloody breaking up. It's never going to last for three days, and that's hundreds of pounds down the pan.'

But Wally Hammond overheard this exchange, and reassured Goddard by saying 'Don't panic Tom, I'll make sure that the match lasts. For a start I'll bat all day on Monday.' True to his word, Hammond batted for over six and a half hours in making a superlative 300, and with 7,000 adoring supporters watching him bat on Monday, Gloucestershire gained a first innings lead of 285. After a composed double hundred, he galloped to 300 in the next seventy minutes, off-driving time and

The Waggon Works ground at Gloucester.

```
                    GLOUCESTERSHIRE v NOTTINGHAMSHIRE

Played at Gloucester on 29th, 31st August, 1st September 1936   Toss: Nottinghamshire
Gloucestershire beat Nottinghamshire by an innings and 70 runs
```

NOTTINGHAMSHIRE

W.W.Keeton		b Stephens	35		lbw	b Cranfield	20
C.B.Harris		b Hammond	6	c	sub	b Stephens	50
W.Walker	c Barnett	b Goddard	6			b Cranfield	9
J.Hardstaff	c Hopkins	b Stephens	46			b Cranfield	0
G.V.Gunn		b Goddard	5			b Goddard	12
A.Staples	c Goddard	b Cranfield	58	c Allen		b Cranfield	52
G.F.H.Heane *	c Page	b Cranfield	11	c Barnett		b Stephens	18
W.Voce		b Cranfield	25			b Barnett	23
F.G.Woodhead	not	out	6	c Stephens		b Barnett	0
A.B.Wheat +	c Stephens	b Goddard	1	c Page		b Barnett	24
H.J.Butler	lbw	b Goddard	0		not	out	3
Extras	(lb 1)		1	(b 3, lb 1)			4
			---				---
TOTAL			200				215

GLOUCESTERSHIRE

C.J.Barnett		b Voce	2
R.W.Haynes	c Staples	b Voce	18
B.O.Allen	c Staples	b Butler	18
W.R.Hammond		b Woodhead	317
W.L.Neale	c Heane	b Butler	66
J.F.Crapp	c Woodhead	b Gunn	22
D.A.C.Page *	lbw	b Heane	8
E.J.Stephens		b Voce	0
T.W.J.Goddard		b Heane	1
V.Hopkins +	not	out	25
L.M.Cranfield	c Wheat	b Staples	0
Extras	(b 6, lb 1, nb 1)		8

TOTAL			485

GLOUCESTERSHIRE	O	M	R	W	O	M	R	W	FALL OF WICKETS			
Hammond	7	0	21	1						N	G	N
Barnett	13	3	51	0	11.3	2	25	3		1st	1st	2nd
Goddard	28.1	9	49	4	25	6	71	1	1st	29	2	25
Stephens	11	0	27	2	8	1	32	2	2nd	43	23	43
Cranfield	23	6	51	3	33	11	71	4	3rd	49	75	43
Haynes					6	1	12	0	4th	66	239	64
									5th	152	322	136
NOTTINGHAMSHIRE									6th	163	345	154
Voce	31	2	117	3					7th	182	346	166
Butler	31	5	79	2					8th	193	351	167
Woodhead	24	3	86	1					9th	196	484	212
Staples	17.4	2	69	1					10th	200	485	215
Gunn	19	3	53	1								
Heane	28	5	73	2								

```
Umpires: W.A.Buswell and G.Brown
```

again with immaculate precision and aplomb. Hammond's 317 was also his best ever score in England and his aggregate that August surpassed the previous record set by W.G. Grace.

To Goddard's great delight another good crowd assembled on the final morning at the Gloucester ground as the visitors tried to save the game. But on a wicket that was increasingly capricious, only Charlie Harris and Arthur Staples offered any lengthy resistance as the Gloucestershire bowlers steadily made their way through the Nottingham batting. The contest ended as Arthur Wheat lobbed a catch into Dallas Page's hands, and the delighted Gloucestershire captain was able to receive the handshakes from the rest of the players before taking his team off the ground. Tragically, this was the final thing he did for Gloucestershire CCC.

WORCESTERSHIRE

7, 9, 10 August 1937 at Cheltenham

'Tom Goddard played his cricket with an uncomplicated passion' – so wrote David Foot, that shrewd and sensitive observer of West Country cricketers. 'He appealed for lbw more than anyone else of his day. The shout was loud, bass-like and with the dogmatic authority of a man who presupposes he will never be turned down!'

A fierce and combative spinner, Goddard waged what at times seemed like a personal battle against a stream of county batsmen, and should one of his appeals, delivered with a lugubrious roar, be turned down, he treated it as a personal slight. As befitted a man of few words, he let the ball do the talking, as it hummed through the air, before tricking and teasing opponents in its deceptive flight or wicked spin and bounce. With his huge fingers wrapped around the ball, Goddard gained appreciable purchase, and his bowling always posed problems for the batsmen, even on the most anodyne of surfaces.

The Cheltenham Festival of 1937 saw Goddard produce one of his finest performances, and all in a season that saw the mighty off-spinner claim 248 wickets, and become one of *Wisden*'s five Cricketers of the Year. The game in question was the local derby against Worcestershire, during which Goddard took all ten wickets in an innings for the first time in his illustrious career.

After taking six wickets in the Worcestershire first innings, Goddard saw his colleagues bat rather indifferently against the visiting bowlers, who secured a 114-run lead for their side. Their efforts though were soon put into context as Goddard started bowling again. Despite some stoic defiance from Harry Gibbons, few of the Worcester men were at ease against the master spinner, whose clever flight and sharp turn confounded a steady procession of batsmen, none of whom were quite certain what the next delivery from Goddard might hold. Some tried to hit their way out of trouble, while others defended stoutly, hoping that occupation of the crease would equate to survival. But all were brushed aside as Goddard steadily worked his way through the Worcestershire line-up, assisted by some outstanding catching close to the wicket and in the deep by the Gloucestershire fielders.

Goddard finished with 10/113, and his magnificent efforts meant that Gloucestershire required 317 to win. Despite his outstanding display, it seemed a mighty mountain to climb on a wicket where the ball was turning and lifting sharply, and it soon became even more daunting as

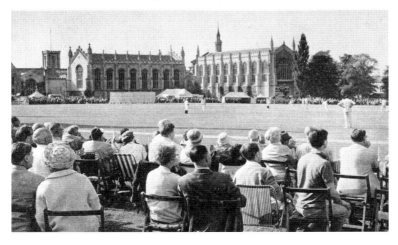

The colleage ground at Cheltenham, with the Gothic Chapel in the background.

```
                    GLOUCESTERSHIRE v WORCESTERSHIRE

Played at Cheltenham College on 7th, 9th, 10th August 1937     Toss: Worcestershire
Gloucestershire beat Worcestershire by 3 wickets

                              WORCESTERSHIRE
C.H.Bull         st Watkins  b Goddard   81     s Watkins    b Goddard  24
J.S.Buller +                 b Lyon      26     c Hammond    b Goddard  12
E.Cooper         c Lyon      b Neale     32                  b Goddard  18
H.H.I.H.Gibbons              b Goddard   36        not          out     72
R.H.C.Human      c Barnett   b Goddard   10 ( 8) c Allen      b Goddard   9
S.H.Martin       hit wicket  b Scott      8     c Hammond    b Goddard   4
B.W.Quaife *                 b Goddard    7 ( 5)              b Goddard   4
R.C.M.Kimpton                b Sinfield  92 ( 7) c Parker     b Goddard   6
R.Howorth        c Parker    b Goddard    6     c Parker     b Goddard   4
R.T.D.Perks                  b Goddard    6     c Crapp      b Goddard  33
P.F.Jackson          not        out       2     c Crapp      b Goddard   3
     Extras      (b 3, lb 1)               4     (b 6, lb 7)            13
                                         ---                           ---
     TOTAL                               310                           202

                              GLOUCESTERSHIRE
C.J.Barnett            lbw    b Jackson   35     c Human      b Perks     9
G.W.Parker                   b Howorth   24 ( 6)    lbw       b Jackson   5
B.O.Allen *      c Buller    b Martin    33     st Buller    b Jackson  78
W.R.Hammond            c & b Howorth      5     c Martin     b Howorth 178
J.F.Crapp                    b Jackson   31                  b Jackson  13
E.K.Scott        c Kimpton   b Howorth    0
R.A.Sinfield     c Kimpton   b Martin    19        not          out      6
B.H.Lyon         c Gibbons   b Howorth    3 ( 2)              b Perks     2
W.L.Neale            not        out      27 ( 8)              b Jackson   1
T.W.J.Goddard    c Perks     b Martin     4 ( 9)    not          out      0
B.T.L.Watkins +              b Jackson    2
     Extras      (b 8, lb 5)              13     (b 11, lb 12, nb 2)     25
                                        ---                            ---
     TOTAL                               196     (for 7 wkts)          317
```

GLOUCESTERSHIRE	O	M	R	W	O	M	R	W	FALL OF WICKETS			
Barnett	5	1	16	0	2	1	5	0		W	G	W	G
Parker	6	1	21	0						1st	1st	2nd	2nd
Lyon	8	3	24	1	2	0	9	0	1st	39	52	25	14
Scott	19	5	42	1	3	0	8	0	2nd	94	74	59	15
Sinfield	24.2	5	82	1	25	7	54	0	3rd	177	98	62	284
Neale	11	2	53	1					4th	194	113	66	302
Goddard	18	4	68	6	28.4	4	113	10	5th	195	121	70	309
									6th	197	139	80	312
WORCESTERSHIRE									7th	223	142	94	314
Perks	6	1	14	0	19	4	52	2	8th	267	190	98	
Martin	7	1	24	3	25	4	67	0	9th	304	194	185	
Human	3	0	5	0					10th	310	196	202	
Howorth	22	4	70	4	26.4	4	76	1					
Jackson	24.5	5	70	3	30	4	92	4					
Kimpton					1	0	5	0					

Umpires: G.M.Lee and F.I.Walden

Gloucestershire's openers were quickly dismissed. But Wally Hammond and Basil Allen then shared a wonderful partnership of 269 for the third wicket to transform a game that had seemed Worcestershire's for the taking.

Hammond's innings was full of glorious and graceful drives, while Allen struck the ball with the kind of power and placement that stemmed from a sharp eye and nimble footwork. Whereas Goddard had ensnared a succession of Worcestershire batsmen, the Gloucestershire batsmen easily broke free from the shackles that the visiting bowlers tried to impose, and in the space of four hours they dramatically turned the game on its head and ensured that Goddard's efforts would not be wasted, as Gloucestershire won by three wickets.

LANCASHIRE

1938 was a red-letter year for Wally Hammond. During a memorable summer that saw him amass over 2,000 runs, he finally achieved what he had long dreamt about – leading England in Test cricket, and in an Ashes series to boot.

This had been Hammond's greatest ambition, and in the minds of many observers, he had charted a singled-minded course during the 1930s towards this goal, carefully choosing his acquaintances among county players and the mandarins at Lord's, as well as dissecting the tactics of many captains with whom he played. But whatever the rights and wrongs of this, Hammond's course of action never ignored the needs of Gloucestershire.

Given the pressures of the Test arena, and the cut and thrust of the battles against the old enemy, many could have forgiven Hammond if he felt slightly jaded when turning out for Gloucestershire in 1938. While many other batsmen might have been happy for others to take centre stage for their county, Hammond never gave anything less than his best for the West Country side during that summer.

An example came at Bristol in mid-July, a fortnight or so after Hammond had struck a regal double century at Lord's in the drawn Second Test. The Third Test at Old Trafford had been washed out without a ball being bowled, so after being cooped up in the Manchester pavilion, it was understandable that Hammond would be eager to spend time in the middle in readiness for the Fourth Test at Headingley.

After watching Cyril Washbrook record an unbeaten double century, Hammond calmly and serenely compiled a fine 200 of his own, and on the third day guided his side past Lancashire's first innings total to secure a lead that the previous day had seemed unlikely as Gloucestershire slipped

Wally Hammond, the England captain, tosses the coin watched by Australian captain Don Bradman and Surrey's groundsman 'Bosser' Martin, at The Oval in 1938.

```
                        GLOUCESTERSHIRE v LANCASHIRE

Played at Bristol on 16th, 18th, 19th July 1938          Toss: Gloucestershire
Match Drawn

                                 LANCASHIRE
C.Washbrook            not               out       219          not            out      51
E.Paynter         c Crapp        b Goddard          60    st Wilson      b Emmett        38
J.Iddon           c Allen        b Goddard           6
N.Oldfield            lbw        b Goddard          20  ( 3)     not            out      13
J.L.Hopwood       c Emmett       b Goddard           2
A.E.Nutter            lbw        b Goddard          17
E.W.Greenhalgh                   b Goddard          36
W.H.L.Lister *    c Crapp        b Sinfield         27
W.Farrimond +                    b Emmett           11
R.Pollard                        b Barnett           5
L.L.Wilkinson         not                out         7
     Extras       (b 15, lb 1)                      16         (b 1, lb 2)               3
                                                   ---                                  ---
     TOTAL              (for 9 wkts dec)           426          (for 1 wkt)            105

                                GLOUCESTERSHIRE
C.J.Barnett       c Pollard      b Iddon           91
B.O.Allen *       c Farrimond    b Greenhalgh       60
W.L.Neale         c Oldfield     b Greenhalgh       11
W.R.Hammond                      b Wilkinson       271
J.F.Crapp                        b Pollard           9
G.M.Emmett                       b Nutter            1
R.W.Haynes            lbw        b Nutter            7
E.D.R.Eagar       c Nutter       b Pollard           0
A.E.Wilson +                     b Hopwood          83
R.A.Sinfield          lbw        b Wilkinson         4
T.W.J.Goddard         not                out         6
     Extras       (b 11, lb 5, nb 2)               18
                                                   ---
     TOTAL                                         561
```

GLOUCESTERSHIRE	O	M	R	W	O	M	R	W	FALL OF WICKETS			
Barnett	13	0	40	1	7	0	20	0		L	G	L
Sinfield	53	10	139	1	10	3	10	0		1st	1st	2nd
Goddard	65	12	144	6					1st	92	152	65
Emmett	28	6	87	1	7	0	14	1	2nd	102	154	
Crapp					7	0	29	0	3rd	134	177	
Haynes					5	0	18	0	4th	138	214	
Neale					3	0	11	0	5th	168	217	
									6th	294	246	
LANCASHIRE									7th	335	263	
Pollard	51	3	163	2					8th	365	502	
Nutter	38	5	92	2					9th	392	536	
Wilkinson	43.4	4	134	2					10th		561	
Iddon	13	3	23	1								
Greenhalgh	22	3	75	2								
Paynter	9	0	31	0								
Hopwood	4	0	25	1								

Umpires: A.Skelding and E.Robinson

to 263 for 7. Any thoughts the visitors may have held about gaining a sizeable lead were brushed aside as Hammond and wicketkeeper Andy Wilson shared a record stand of 239 for the eighth wicket.

Hammond completely dominated the stand and as the doughty 'keeper later said 'He told me to run when he called me – and there was a spell when I don't think I got a ball for six overs!' After reaching his hundred in three and a quarter hours, he soberly went on past 200 and in the process reached the landmark of 2,000 runs for the season before being bowled by Len Wilkinson.

His efforts had helped to save a game that the previous night had seemed in the balance for the Gloucestershire side, and as far as England were concerned, his magnificent innings was evidence that their captain was in fine form for the second half of their Ashes challenge.

When asked to choose Wally Hammond's finest innings on a treacherous wicket, his contemporaries would have had little hesitation in choosing his unbeaten 153 against Kent at Bristol in 1939.

If ever his genius with the bat needed a demonstration, this match was the perfect showcase, with the ball turning in a quite fiendish way on a dry and dusty surface where the odd delivery was also keeping wickedly low. Had a modern-day Pitch Liaison Officer been present, he would have quickly been on the phone to speak to Lord's. That is until Hammond was on strike, because when Wally was facing it looked a completely different and very easy game.

Right from the outset, good fortune was on Hammond's side as he won the toss for the first time in thirteen attempts. But luck had no part to play when it came to batting, and in order to survive on this fiendish wicket, it took batting skill of the highest calibre. As Andy Wilson, the Gloucestershire wicketkeeper later wrote, 'while the rest of the team pushed and prodded like old ladies at a jumble sale, Wally treated the pitch as if it were a perfect batting strip. Everything was played with absolute confidence in the middle of the bat. Almost every batsman in that match was made to look like a novice, but Wally showed complete mastery.'

After adding a forthright 125 with Charlie Barnett for the third wicket, Hammond carefully shielded his later partners from the crafty leg-spin of Doug Wright, who despite Hammond's best efforts gradually disposed of his partners. His reward was a career-best 9/47 and a hat-trick to finish off the Gloucestershire resistance, but when the last wicket fell, Hammond was still there, agonisingly marooned at the non-striker's end, with a majestic 153 to his name – over half of his side's total of 284.

The second day then saw Tom Goddard equal the world record by taking seventeen wickets in the day's play as Kent were dismissed twice and beaten by an innings as the ball continued to lift and bounce, almost at right angles. In taking seventeen wickets in a day, he emulated the feats of

Charlie Barnett batting in Australia for England on their 1936/37 tour.

```
                        GLOUCESTERSHIRE v KENT

Played at Bristol on 1st, 3rd July 1939            Toss: Gloucestershire
Gloucestershire beat Kent by an innings and 40 runs

                              GLOUCESTERSHIRE
R.A.Sinfield              c & b Longfield    15
C.J.Barnett        lbw      b Wright         66
V.Hopkins                 c & b Wright        2
W.R.Hammond *             not     out       153
J.F.Crapp          c Levett  b Wright         4
G.M.Emmett         lbw      b Wright          0
W.L.Neale          lbw      b Wright          0
A.E.Wilson +               b Wright         10
R.W.Haynes                 b Wright         16
G.E.E.Lambert              b Wright          0
T.W.J.Goddard      lbw      b Wright          0
     Extras        (b 7, lb 10, nb 1)       18
                                           ---
     TOTAL                                  284

                                   KENT
A.E.Fagg                  b Goddard    8 ( 3) c Hammond   b Goddard    33
F.G.H.Chalk *   c Neale    b Goddard   40          lbw    b Sinfield   21
L.E.G.Ames         lbw     b Lambert   12 ( 1) c Haynes   b Goddard    16
B.H.Valentine   c Crapp    b Goddard   14        c Hopkins b Sinfield   0
L.J.Todd                   b Goddard   15        c Barnett b Goddard    2
T.W.Spencer                b Goddard    0          lbw    b Goddard    15
T.C.Longfield              b Goddard    0        c Emmett  b Goddard    14
D.V.P.Wright               b Goddard    0        st Wilson b Goddard     2
N.W.Harding        not      out        19        c Emmett  b Goddard    13
W.H.V.Levett +             b Goddard    8          not      out         3
C.Lewis                    b Goddard    0        c Haynes  b Goddard     5
     Extras        (b 2, lb 2)           4
                                       ---                            ---
     TOTAL                              120                            124

KENT             O    M    R    W     O    M    R    W    FALL OF WICKETS
Harding         12    3   39    0                          G    K    K
Todd            25    2  111    0                         1st  1st  2nd
Longfield       14    3   40    1                    1st   36   30   21
Wright          21.5  8   47    9                    2nd   43   53   38
Lewis            8    0   29    0                    3rd  168   73   46
                                                     4th  180   77   53
GLOUCESTERSHIRE                                      5th  180   77   73
Barnett          2    0    9    0     1    0    6    0    6th  180   87   93
Lambert          8    1   40    1     6    1   19    0    7th  212   87  103
Goddard         15.4  2   38    9    16.2  1   68    8    8th  284   96  116
Sinfield         9    2   29    0    12    3   31    2    9th  284  120  117
                                                    10th  284  120  124

Umpires: H.G.Baldwin and H.Cruice
```

Hedley Verity in 1933 and Colin Blythe in 1907, and although the newspapers were starting to forecast the outbreak of war, it was the amazing feats of Goddard and Hammond that were the main topic of conversation in the pubs of Bristol in July 1939.

Tom Goddard was never an easy bowler to face, and on this particular track, few of the visitors were at ease against him. There was no Hammond in the Kent ranks and despite the efforts of their captain Gerry Chalk, no Kent batsman got past 40. As Goddard worked his way through their batting to reach his century of victims for the summer, how Kent must have wished that they had been successful back in the 1920s in regaining the services of the Dover-born batsman. Had they done so, what a wonderful contest this might have been between a master bowler and a genius with the bat.

YORKSHIRE

Sam Cook (opposite) was always held in high regard by Gloucestershire's officials. 'I reckon this fellow will take a hundred wickets this year,' remarked their captain Wally Hammond to a watching committee member as the unknown twenty-four-year-old left-arm spinner wheeled away in the nets at Bristol after signing for the county at the start of the 1946 season. 'And I think he'll play for England one day!'

Hammond was clearly a fine judge because in his debut season, Cook claimed 113 Championship wickets, as well as winning his county cap and a place in the second Test Trial at Canterbury. His star was certainly in the ascendancy and in mid-May the following year, the phlegmatic Cook took 6/44 as the MCC defeated the South Africans at Lord's. A fortnight later Cook took a remarkable 9/42 for Gloucestershire against Yorkshire at Bristol in a career-best performance that also resulted in Cook's selection for the opening Test against the Springboks at Trent Bridge.

This classic match against Yorkshire at Bristol began on a wicket that had been freshened up by overnight rain, and Cook's accurate spin put a brake on the Tykes progress after Willie Watson and Norman Yardley had added 77 for the second wicket. But Cook dismissed both batsmen in an amazing spell that saw him take 9/19 in the space of 15 overs, including the last four wickets without conceding a run, to the delight of a home crowd of around 10,000.

Charlie Barnett, who had chosen the contest as his benefit match, then proved that batting was perfectly possible, caressing the ball to the cover boundary as well as driving powerfully off his legs in scoring a bold 70 as Gloucestershire gained a 48-run lead. After his stunning first-innings performance Cook went wicketless a second time around, and it was Tom Goddard, the wily old veteran, who posed all manner of problems for the visitors as the wicket gave increasing assistance to the spinners.

Goddard's 6/35 meant that the home county only required 71 to win and after a breezy opening stand by Barnett and Basil Allen, Gloucestershire romped to victory before the close of the second day. It meant that Barnett was deprived of a third day's takings, but a collection on the opening day raised £170, and there was another broad smile on Barnett's face, as well as those of the

```
                      GLOUCESTERSHIRE v YORKSHIRE

Played at Bristol on 31st May, 2nd June 1947           Toss: Yorkshire
Gloucestershire beat Yorkshire by 9 wickets

                                YORKSHIRE
L.Hutton              b Barnett    4        c & b Lambert       1
W.Watson              b Cook      52    c Wilcox  b Goddard    26
N.W.D.Yardley  c Crapp b Cook     43    c Goddard b Barnett    58
J.V.Wilson     c Crapp b Cook      4    c Allen   b Barnett     0
F.Jakeman      c Crapp b Cook      1    st Wilson b Goddard     2
A.B.Sellers *  c Allen b Cook      0    c Neale   b Goddard    16
T.F.Smailes    st Wilson b Cook   16    st Wilson b Goddard     0
H.Crick +      c Lyon  b Cook      7              b Barnett     3
A.Mason               b Cook       0         not  out           0
E.P.Robinson      not   out        0              b Goddard     4
W.E.Bowes      st Wilson b Cook    0    c Crapp   b Goddard     0
    Extras     (b 1)               1    (b 4, lb 5)             9
                                 ---                         ---
    TOTAL                         128                         119

                             GLOUCESTERSHIRE
C.J.Barnett           b Smailes   70         not   out         30
B.O.Allen *    c Crick b Smailes  19    st Crick  b Robinson   31
W.L.Neale      st Crick b Smailes  8         not   out          1
J.F.Crapp      c Bowes b Robinson 11
G.M.Emmett            b Robinson   3
B.H.Lyon              b Robinson  10
A.E.Wilson +   c Yardley b Smailes 11
A.G.S.Wilcox   c Smailes b Robinson 12
G.E.E.Lambert         b Smailes    1
T.W.J.Goddard       c & b Smailes 16
C.Cook           not   out         2
    Extras     (b 11, lb 2)       13    (b 10)                 10
                                 ---                         ---
    TOTAL                         176    (for 1 wkt)           72
```

GLOUCESTERSHIRE	O	M	R	W	O	M	R	W	FALL OF WICKETS				
Lambert	6	2	23	0	1	0	9	1		Y	G	Y	G
Barnett	7	3	14	1	13	3	33	3		1st	1st	2nd	2nd
Cook	22.5	7	42	9	10	1	33	0	1st	5	40	1	71
Goddard	21	6	48	0	12.5	3	35	6	2nd	82	52	91	
									3rd	88	72	94	
YORKSHIRE									4th	94	84	96	
Bowes	4	2	10	0	3	0	7	0	5th	96	102	102	
Smailes	21.2	7	42	6	7	1	18	0	6th	109	134	102	
Mason	17	8	45	0					7th	125	149	111	
Robinson	22	8	66	4	6.5	0	37	1	8th	125	154	115	
									9th	128	157	119	
									10th	128	176	119	

Umpires: J.J.Hills and C.N.Woolley

Gloucestershire supporters, when news came through of Cook's selection for the First Test at Nottingham.

It turned out to be Cook's only appearance for England, and on the featherbed wicket, he lost his customary accuracy to finish with 0/127 in 30 overs. How different it might have been had the match been staged on the sandy wickets at Bristol: as one county player once said, 'With Cookie at one end and big Tom Goddard at the other, what chance did a batsman have at Bristol just after the war unless he had a bucket and spade with him!'

MIDDLESEX

16, 18 August 1947 at Cheltenham

To the delight of their many supporters, 1947 saw Gloucestershire mount a concerted bid for the County Championship title. Such riches seemed light years away as the season began with Wally Hammond announcing his retirement from county cricket after returning from the winter tour to Australia, before Gloucestershire subsided to an innings defeat against Middlesex at Lord's in their opening Championship fixture of the season.

But by the time the two counties met up again, at the Cheltenham Festival in mid-August, the situation was very different. Basil Allen's team had recorded no less than fourteen victories and were neck-and-neck with Middlesex in the race for the county title, and the game at the College Ground was likely to determine the outcome of the County Championship. Aware of this, a record crowd of 14,500 crammed into the Cheltenham ground on the first day, and the gates had to be shut, leaving many disappointed supporters left outside.

The mood in the Gloucestershire camp was high, especially as Middlesex had arrived at the Cotswold town without either Denis Compton or Jack Robertson who had been chosen for England in the Fifth Test against the South Africans at The Oval. But the visitors still had many fine batsmen, and Syd Brown with Bill Edrich launched the Middlesex innings adding a composed half-century stand, before the Gloucestershire spinners made their way through the Middlesex innings. Tom Goddard, the forty-six-year-old sorcerer, and his twenty-five-year-old apprentice Sam Cook, brought a smile to the faces of their many supporters as Middlesex were dismissed for 180.

But batting was still difficult when the home team began their reply, and despite the urgings of the partisan crowd, Jim Sims and Jack Young showed their liking for the Cheltenham wicket. Only Jack Crapp, the thirty-four-year-old Cornishman, and George Emmett offered any resistance, as Middlesex secured a slender first innings lead of 27.

The second day saw the spinners in the ascendancy again, and also one of the finest catches in Gloucestershire's history after Walter Robins, the Middlesex captain, had attempted to counter-attack against the home bowlers. He smashed 45 in forty-nine minutes, before attempting another huge leg-side hit off Goddard. It looked like being a certain six, but Cliff Monks, the thirty-five-year-

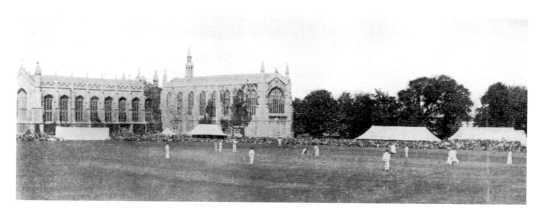

The College ground in Festival week.

GLOUCESTERSHIRE COUNTY CRICKET MATCHES

to be played in Cheltenham on the College Ground.

WED., THURS. and FRI., AUG. 13th, 14th and 15th.

GLOUCESTERSHIRE v. SOUTH AFRICA

SAT., MON. and TUES., AUG. 16th, 18th and 19th.

GLOUCESTERSHIRE v. MIDDLESEX

WED., THURS. and FRI., AUG. 20th, 21st and 22nd.

GLOUCESTERSHIRE v. GLAMORGAN

PLAY - MON., WED., THURS. & SAT., 11.30 a.m. to 6.30 p.m.
TUES. & FRI., 11.30 a.m. to 6 p.m.
(Extra half-hour on third day if necessary).
LUNCH INTERVAL 1.30 p.m. to 2.10 p.m.

Charges: Admission 2/-; Enclosure 2/- extra.   Admission after 4 p.m. 1/-
Juveniles (under 14) 1/- (All including Tax).

Car Park 2/- (Sandford Mill Farm, Old Bath Road).

Season Tickets obtainable from W. A. WOOF LTD., Regent Street, Cheltenham.

The Gloucestershire team of 1947.

old all-rounder raced along the boundary rope from long-on. Even though many spectators had spilled onto the field, Monks held both his concentration and a stunning head-high catch, never once showing any hesitation in his stride and holding onto the ball with one hand outstretched in front of the enraptured crowd. It seemed almost as if he had plucked the ball from the midst of the spectators, and as Robins started to head back to the pavilion, he stood for a moment and joined in with the applause and cheers by tapping his bat in recognition of Monks' outstanding efforts.

But Harry Sharp, playing in his first match of the summer, took up the reins and despatched Goddard for 8 fours, all of which were played with great skill through the leg-side. Goddard eventually gained his revenge, dismissing the Middlesex man 4 runs away from a much-deserved half-century.

The last six wickets then fell for 16 runs, as Goddard finished with 8 wickets to his name, and the outcome was that Gloucestershire needed 169 to win, and defeat their rivals for the Championship title.

How they must have wished that they had the experience of Wally Hammond to call upon, on a wicket that was increasingly misbehaving and assisting the spinners in true Cheltenham tradition.

George Emmett

GLOUCESTERSHIRE v MIDDLESEX

Played at Cheltenham College on 16th, 18th August 1947   Toss: Middlesex
Middlesex beat Gloucestershire by 68 runs

MIDDLESEX

S.M.Brown	lbw	b Scott	15 (2)		b Goddard	11
W.J.Edrich	c Allen	b Cook	50 (1)	lbw	b Goddard	5
F.G.Mann	c Crapp	b Goddard	8 (5)	st Wilson	b Goddard	7
R.W.V.Robins *	c Scott	b Goddard	2	c Monks	b Goddard	45
A.W.Thompson		b Goddard	2 (6)	lbw	b Goddard	1
J.P.Mann	c Lambert	b Goddard	7 (7)	lbw	b Cook	5
L.H.Compton +	lbw	b Goddard	3 (8)	c Barnett	b Goddard	3
J.M.Sims	c Allen	b Goddard	32 (9)	c Neale	b Goddard	5
H.P.H.Sharp	not	out	14 (3)	c Barnett	b Goddard	46
L.H.Gray	lbw	b Cook	0 (11)	not	out	0
J.A.Young		b Goddard	27 (10)	c Wilson	b Cook	0
Extras	(b 11, lb 7, nb 2)		20	(b 4, lb 9)		13
TOTAL			180			141

GLOUCESTERSHIRE

C.J.Barnett	c Young	b Sims	19	lbw	b Young	17
B.O.Allen *	c Gray	b Sims	20	c sub	b Sims	10
W.L.Neale	c Sharp	b Sims	4	c sub	b Sharp	10
J.F.Crapp		c & b Young	10	c Robins	b Young	40
G.M.Emmett	lbw	b Young	33	c Compton	b Sharp	0
C.I.Monks	lbw	b Sims	4 (7)	c Brown	b Young	4
A.E.Wilson +	not	out	17 (6)	c Compton	b Sharp	0
G.E.E.Lambert	lbw	b Young	5		b Young	1
C.J.Scott		b Sims	1	st Compton	b Sims	8
T.W.J.Goddard		c & b Sims	26	c Edrich	b Young	0
C.Cook		b Young	1	not	out	0
Extras	(b 10, lb 1, nb 2)		13	(b 6, lb 4)		10
TOTAL			153			100

GLOUCESTERSHIRE	O	M	R	W	O	M	R	W
Barnett	4	0	15	0	3	1	6	0
Lambert	8	2	19	0	1	0	1	0
Scott	5	0	15	1				
Cook	21	9	41	2	18.5	8	35	2
Goddard	20.3	4	70	7	22	4	86	8
MIDDLESEX								
Gray	2	0	10	0				
Young	25.1	8	55	4	19	9	27	5
Sims	22	4	65	6	9.3	2	24	2
Robins	3	0	10	0				
Sharp					9	0	39	3

FALL OF WICKETS

	M	G	M	G
	1st	1st	2nd	2nd
1st	50	37	5	22
2nd	65	44	33	32
3rd	77	49	103	67
4th	92	91	125	67
5th	94	100	128	69
6th	101	100	129	74
7th	112	106	135	91
8th	140	107	141	96
9th	143	152	141	100
10th	180	153	141	100

Umpires: H.Cruice and H.Elliott

Jack Young needed no second invitation, and with Sharp's off-spinners getting bite out of the wicket, the crowd, who had started the day in an expectant mood, saw their hopes and dreams dashed as Gloucestershire were dismissed for exactly 100.

The victory gave the Middlesex side the boost they needed in the final fortnight of the season, and their defeat ended Gloucestershire's brave title bid. As hard as they tried, Basil Allen's team could not regain the ground they had lost during the closing games of the summer, and they ended the summer 20 points behind Middlesex as Championship runners-up.

AUSTRALIANS

After their classic encounter with the 1930 Australians, fixtures against the men with the baggy green caps always held a special attraction to the supporters of Gloucestershire. The arrival of Don Bradman's men in Bristol in 1948 – the centenary of the birth of W.G. – was met with an enormous crowd at the Nevil Road ground, and the contest was staged in front of a record 15,000 spectators.

Many had turned up in the hope of seeing Bradman bat again at Bristol, but as on the previous two tours, he opted to sit on the sidelines, perhaps remembering the way that Tom Goddard had tied him up in knots on the 1930 tour. The tall veteran was still in the Gloucestershire side, but on this occasion he was rendered innocuous as the Australians rattled up 774 for 7 – the highest total of the summer, the best by an Australian team against an English county and the highest score ever made against Gloucestershire.

The opening day belonged almost solely to left-handed opener Arthur Morris, who struck a century before lunch, reached his double hundred before tea, and was poised to complete a triple hundred before the close when he was caught and bowled by Colin Scott, the blond-haired fast bowler from Downend Cricket Club. Sam Loxton also made an unbeaten 159 as the home bowlers tired, driving four huge sixes, while Neil Harvey made a carefree 95 before falling to Sam Cook 5 runs short of a richly deserved and entertaining century.

When the tourists bowled, few of the Gloucestershire batsmen offered any lengthy resistance, and the Australians strolled to a comfortable victory. Jack Crapp (above) was the notable exception, and for around three-and-a-half hours in the first innings he stoutly defied the visitors' attack. The Aussies were very mindful of the fact that Crapp had been called up to make his England debut for Third Test at Old Trafford, so his innings at Bristol gave them a chance to assess the Cornishman's strengths and weaknesses. As he reached his century, there were a few verbal exchanges with the Australians, who left him in no doubt what to expect at Manchester – 'Well played Jack,' said Keith Miller, 'but you had better watch your head in the Test.'

True to his word, Miller let rip at Crapp, who had walked out to the crease at Old Trafford proudly wearing his England cap for the first time, after Denis Compton had been felled by a bouncer from Ray Lindwall and been forced to retire hurt. It spoke volumes for his composure that

```
                    GLOUCESTERSHIRE v AUSTRALIANS

Played at Bristol on 3rd, 5th, 6th July 1948           Toss: Australians
Australians beat Gloucestershire by an innings and 363 runs

                              AUSTRALIANS
S.G.Barnes      c Crapp        b Cook          44
A.R.Morris                 c & b Scott        290
A.L.Hassett *   st Wilson      b Cook          21
K.R.Miller      c Cook         b Scott         51
R.N.Harvey      c Allen        b Cook          95
S.J.E.Loxton         not             out      159
C.L.McCool                     b Barnett       76
I.W.Johnson                c & b Hale          27
R.R.Lindwall         not             out        0
R.A.Saggers +
D.T.Ring
    Extras      (b 4, lb 6, w 1)               11
                                              ---
    TOTAL              (for 7 wkts dec)       774
```

```
                            GLOUCESTERSHIRE
G.M.Emmett      c Lindwall   b Johnson    43                 b Ring         9
B.O.Allen *              c & b Johnson    31   c Harvey      b Johnson     34
C.J.Barnett     c Lindwall   b Ring       10                 b Ring         4
J.F.Crapp           not           out    100   c Saggers     b Johnson     32
C.I.Monks                    b Ring        1   c Harvey      b Johnson      5
A.E.Wilson +    c Barnes      b Loxton     46                 b Ring        10
I.E.Hale                     b Johnson      3   c Ring       b Johnson      4
L.M.Cranfield       lbw       b Morris     23   c Morris     b Ring         1
C.J.Scott       st Saggers    b Johnson     2   st Saggers   b Ring         3
T.W.J.Goddard   c Saggers     b Johnson     0       not         out       10
C.Cook                        b Johnson     5   st Saggers   b Johnson     13
    Extras      (b 9, lb 5, nb 1)          15   (b 4, lb 3)                 7
                                          ---                             ---
    TOTAL                                 279                             132
```

```
GLOUCESTERSHIRE   O    M    R    W      O    M    R    W     FALL OF WICKETS
Barnett          24    2  102    1                             A    G    G
Scott            31    2  172    2                           1st  1st  2nd
Monks             9    1   32    0                      1st   102   74   16
Goddard          32    3  186    0                      2nd   168   79   20
Cook             41    6  147    3                      3rd   304   87   72
Cranfield        23    4  106    0                      4th   466   90   80
Hale              3    0   18    1                      5th   529  175   93
                                                       6th   669  187  100
AUSTRALIANS                                            7th   774  257  101
Lindwall         18    4   36    0      3    1    5    0   8th        267  109
Loxton            9    2   22    1      2    0    2    0   9th        267  109
Johnson        31.4   12   68    6   17.1    6   32    5  10th        279  132
Ring             25    3   83    2     25    9   47    5
McCool           10    0   35    0      9    5   16    0
Morris            4    0   20    1      9    3   15    0
Hassett                                 2    0    8    0

Umpires: F.S.Lee and K.McCanlis
```

Crapp held his nerve and calmly played himself in, against some hostile bowling from the Australians. But Miller had not forgotten his exchange with Crapp at Bristol, and in the Fifth Test at The Oval he struck Crapp a fearsome blow on his head that left the doughty left-hander with a headache for many days.

DERBYSHIRE

In 1949, Ken Graveney, the elder brother of Tom, became only the fourth bowler in Gloucestershire's history to take all ten wickets in an innings, with 10/66 against Derbyshire at Chesterfield. They were also the second-best bowling figures in the club's long history, and all on a Queens Park wicket that was expected to give assistance to the spinners.

In fact, Ken nearly didn't get a chance to bowl when Derbyshire batted 352 runs in arrears towards the end of the first day. The Gloucestershire captain Basil Allen intended to immediately bring on his spin bowlers, but after a few words from some of the senior players, Allen decided to let the seamers have a few overs, primarily to get the shine off the ball. With the penultimate ball of his second over, Graveney claimed his first wicket, so Allen decided to give him another over in the hope that he might claim a further rather unexpected victim. Graveney did his captain proud by taking a wicket in his third, fourth and fifth over to finish the day's play with figures of 4 wickets for 5 runs.

The following morning, he added another scalp in the opening over of the morning, and then added another four in his subsequent overs. Derbyshire's final pair, Bill Copson and Les Jackson, then offered stout resistance, and as they dug in, Allen told Graveney he would have only three more overs in which to take his tenth wicket. But Graveney did not miss out on a place in Gloucestershire's record books, as Copson holed out at extra cover to give the young bowler his prized haul.

This was to prove to be Graveney's finest hour for Gloucestershire as the following year, he started to suffer from disc problems in his back, and in 1951 he retired from first-class cricket. He returned to the game ten years later, initially as Second XI captain, but then after Tom Pugh's retirement, Graveney led the county side in 1963 and 1964 before handing over the reins to John Mortimore.

Ken Graveney: a 'ten for' at Chesterfield.

DERBYSHIRE v GLOUCESTERSHIRE

Played at Chesterfield on 3rd, 4th, 5th August 1949   Toss: Gloucestershire
Gloucestershire beat Derbyshire by 184 runs

GLOUCESTERSHIRE

G.M.Emmett	c Dawkes	b Jackson	34		b Carr	92
T.W.Graveney		b Gladwin	0 (3)	lbw	b Gladwin	15
B.O.Allen *	lbw	b Copson	1 (2)	c Sale	b Gladwin	60
J.F.Crapp	c Dawkes	b Gladwin	30	c Revill	b Gladwin	33
C.A.Milton	not	out	92	c & b Carr		14
A.E.Wilson +	c Dawkes	b Gladwin	0		b Gladwin	36
C.I.Monks	c Eggar	b Gladwin	0		b Carr	7
G.E.E.Lambert	c Eggar	b Gladwin	0	c Eggar	b Carr	16
J.K.R.Graveney	c Gladwin	b Rhodes	0	c Eggar	b Carr	1
T.W.J.Goddard	run	out	20	st Dawkes	b Carr	13
C.Cook	lbw	b Rhodes	18	not	out	2
Extras	(lb 3)		3	(b 9, lb 4)		13
TOTAL			198			302

DERBYSHIRE

R.Sale		b J.K.R.Graveney	12		b J.K.R.Graveney	7
C.S.Elliott	c Wilson	b Cook	34	c Crapp	b J.K.R.Graveney	1
A.C.Revill		b Lambert	1		b J.K.R.Graveney	0
J.D.Eggar	lbw	b Goddard	21	c Allen	b J.K.R.Graveney	14
D.B.Carr	lbw	b Cook	0	c & b J.K.R.Graveney		0
A.E.G.Rhodes	lbw	b Cook	42	c T.W.Graveney	b J.K.R.Graveney	65
D.A.Skinner *		b Goddard	1	c Goddard	b J.K.R.Graveney	39
C.Gladwin	c Crapp	b Cook	18 (9)		b J.K.R.Graveney	8
G.O.Dawkes +		b Goddard	0 (8)	c Lambert	b J.K.R.Graveney	9
W.H.Copson		b Cook	11	c Emmett	b J.K.R.Graveney	2
H.L.Jackson	not	out	0	not	out	5
Extras	(b 1, lb 8)		9	(b 10, lb 1, w 4, nb 2)		17
TOTAL			149			167

DERBYSHIRE	O	M	R	W	O	M	R	W	FALL OF WICKETS				
										G	D	G	D
Copson	17	3	50	1	5	0	24	0		1st	1st	2nd	2nd
Gladwin	27	13	53	5	38	11	92	4	1st	8	30	130	8
Jackson	22	8	40	1	8	1	32	0	2nd	15	31	169	10
Rhodes	10.5	0	52	2	9	2	30	0	3rd	60	55	173	13
Carr					24.2	3	111	6	4th	68	55	201	13
									5th	78	117	231	88
DERBYSHIRE									6th	86	119	243	108
Lambert	16	4	48	1	16	2	51	0	7th	86	126	285	118
J.K.R.Graveney	9	1	28	1	18.4	2	66	10	8th	91	132	287	137
Cook	15.1	4	40	5	2	0	12	0	9th	135	144	287	158
Goddard	9	2	24	3	5	0	21	0	10th	198	149	302	167

Umpires: H.W.Parks and E.Cooke

SOMERSET

4, 6, 7 August 1956 at Taunton

There have been many intense local derbies between Gloucestershire and Somerset, but this encounter at Taunton in 1956 saw Gloucestershire batting second and win by the narrowest possible margin of one wicket, thanks to a stirring tenth-wicket partnership by Sam Cook and Peter Rochford as Gloucestershire chased 161 in 132 minutes on the final day.

Neither Cook or Rochford were renowned for their batting abilities, with Cook for many years having more career wickets than runs to his name. He had struck two hundreds, albeit in rather unconventional manner, in minor games while on National Service, and during his county career he had shown a penchant for a rather rustic flail, dubbed the 'Tetbury Chop', which colleagues rather unflattering described as bearing a close resemblance to the sort of blow a rat catcher would make!

Rochford had joined the Gloucestershire staff in 1952 initially as an understudy to the great Andy Wilson, before taking over as first-choice wicketkeeper in 1954. However, it was for his deft glove-work, rather than his abilities as a batsman, that he won a regular place in the Gloucestershire side, but in this classic match Rochford helped Cook to score the 18 runs that were needed when they came together with the match on a knife-edge, and the minutes ticking away. While Rochford propped forward, Cook unfurled his favourite chop stroke, and to the delight of the visiting supporters, 10 runs came from an over from John McMahon, and Gloucestershire scrambled home with one wicket in hand.

It had certainly been a good match for Cook, who took eleven wickets in the game. In Somerset's second innings, he troubled all of their batsmen with his guile and cunning, and in typical fashion,

'Bomber' Wells

Peter Rochford

```
                    SOMERSET v GLOUCESTERSHIRE

Played at Taunton on 4th, 6th, 7th August 1956          Toss: Somerset
Gloucestershire beat Somerset by 1 wicket

                              SOMERSET
L.Pickles          c Graveney   b Wells       53    c Emmett     b Cook      39
J.G.Lomax          c Rochford   b Lambert      1    c Crapp      b Wells      9
P.B.Wight               c & b Wells           12          lbw   b Wells     12
C.L.McCool         c Rochford   b Cook        88    c Rochford  b Cook      57
G.Atkinson              c & b Wells            0 ( 6)        lbw b Cook      43
M.F.Tremlett *     c Milton     b Cook         0 ( 7) c Young   b Wells      7
H.W.Stephenson +   c Graveney   b Cook        22 ( 5) c Milton  b Cook       1
J.Hilton              not        out          39          not   out         9
P.H.Fussell        c Graveney   b Cook         0          b Wells           0
J.W.J.McMahon                   b Lake        10          lbw   b Cook       9
B.Lobb                          b Cook         8                b Cook       2
     Extras         (b 8, lb 4, nb 1)         13    (b 12, lb 1)            13
                                             ---                           ---
     TOTAL                                    246                           201

                           GLOUCESTERSHIRE
C.A.Milton         c Wight      b McMahon    138    c Wight     b McMahon    26
D.M.Young                       b Lobb        81    c Tremlett  b Lomax       7
G.M.Emmett *           run        out          2    c McCool    b McMahon    55
T.W.Graveney       c McCool     b Hilton      29    c Stephenson b McMahon    6
J.F.Crapp             not        out          23 ( 6)          b Hilton     31
G.E.E.Lambert         not        out           3 ( 7) c Hilton b McCool      2
J.B.Mortimore                                    ( 5) c Hilton  b McCool      5
G.J.Lake                                            c Stephenson b McCool     7
B.D.Wells                                           c Wight     b Hilton      0
P.Rochford +                                            not     out          5
C.Cook                                                 not      out         13
     Extras         (b 3, lb 4, w 4)          11    (b 1, lb 3)              4
                                             ---                           ---
     TOTAL          (for 4 wkts dec)         287    (for 9 wkts)           161
```

GLOUCESTERSHIRE	O	M	R	W	O	M	R	W	FALL OF WICKETS				
											S	G	S	G
Lambert	21	4	57	1	6	0	22	0						
Lake	12	2	30	1	2	1	2	0			1st 1st 2nd 2nd			
Wells	26	13	54	3	37	9	83	4	1st	9	209	37	14
Cook	30.5	12	64	5	29.2	13	53	6	2nd	30	226	60	69
Mortimore	8	1	28	0	5	0	14	0	3rd	154	243	70	82
Graveney					3	0	14	0	4th	155	268	71	97
									5th	160		156	107
SOMERSET									6th	160		181	126
Lobb	31	7	69	1	5.2	0	18	0	7th	186		183	138
Fussell	16	3	45	0					8th	186		184	138
McCool	7	0	39	0	13	1	35	3	9th	210		193	143
McMahon	27	7	69	1	14	1	52	3	10th	246		201	
Hilton	19	10	33	1	6	0	27	2					
Lomax	7	2	21	0	5	0	25	1					

Umpires: W.T.Jones and C.S.Elliott

dismissed six batsmen, each time with a wicked smile on his face. 1956 proved to be Cook's most successful season in his illustrious career, with the left-arm spinner claiming 149 wickets at just 14 apiece, and it spoke volumes for the luxury of riches at England's disposal that they could consistently overlook the claims of the 'Tetbury Twirler'.

WARWICKSHIRE

12, 13, 14 June 1957 at Edgbaston

The years after the Second World War had seen the curtain finally fall on Wally Hammond's illustrious career, but the golden post-war summers also witnessed the birth of a new batting star in Gloucestershire's rank – Tom Graveney; a man whose graceful and elegant stroke-play could stand fair comparison with that of Hammond in the 1920s and 1930s.

Like his predecessor, Graveney was born outside the county – in his case Northumberland – but educated inside the county's boundaries – at Bristol Grammar School – where he proved himself to be a natural sportsman. In 1948 he also turned down an offer to become an accountant, and accepted instead a place on the county's staff. He soon proved that it had been a very wise decision, and in every summer between 1949 and 1960 Graveney passed a 1,000 runs, and cheered the county's supporters with some exquisite batting.

England honours duly came his way from 1951, and this classic match in 1957 at Edgbaston highlighted his prodigious technique, and an ability to score runs when others failed. It was also a game that saw Graveney become the first batsman to reach 1,000 runs for the summer, and in a match when only one of his colleagues passed fifty in the contest, his own match aggregate was 207.

In the first innings, Graveney struck a typically graceful 106, made out of 130 runs while he was at the crease. His two-hour innings was finally ended by a ball from Ray Carter, but not before Graveney had attacked with gusto the wily leg-breaks and googlies of Eric Hollies, who claimed six wickets. Second time around, Graveney's batting was even more impressive, playing with superb care and immaculate timing against the sharply turning deliveries of Hollies and Billy Ibadulla. No less than 80 out of his 101 runs came from boundaries, as Graveney pierced the field with his strokes.

Tom Graveney

```
                        WARWICKSHIRE v GLOUCESTERSHIRE

Played at Birmingham on 12th, 13th, 14th June 1957        Toss: Gloucestershire
Warwickshire beat Gloucestershire by 6 wickets

                              GLOUCESTERSHIRE
G.M.Emmett *                b Hollies      52    c Spooner   b Ibadulla    25
D.M.Young          c Smith   b Hollies      29       lbw    b Hollies      18
W.Knightley-Smith  c Spooner b Hollies       4    c Singh   b Ibadulla     16
T.W.Graveney       c Townsend b Carter      106      not       out        101
R.B.Nicholls       c Cartwright b Hollies    14      lbw    b Ibadulla      8
J.B.Mortimore      c Townsend b Ibadulla      2    c Townsend b Ibadulla    4
B.J.Meyer +        c Spooner b Carter        13      lbw    b Bannister     8
G.G.M.Wiltshire             b Bannister      18    c Townsend b Singh      14
D.R.Smith          c Smith   b Hollies       15    c Smith   b Singh       14
C.Cook                not       out           2      lbw    b Hollies       0
B.D.Wells       hit wicket b Hollies         13      lbw    b Hollies       6
     Extras       (lb 2)                      2    (b 4, lb 2, nb 1)        7
                                            ---                           ---
     TOTAL                                   270                           221

                               WARWICKSHIRE
F.C.Gardner        c Knightley-Smith b Cook  163      not       out         73
N.F.Horner         c Graveney b Cook          29      run       out          4
M.J.K.Smith *      c Smith   b Graveney       59    c Young   b Wells        0
A.Townsend                  b Graveney         0           c & b Mortimore  12
T.W.Cartwright     c Graveney b Wiltshire     22            b Mortimore      2
R.T.Spooner +      c Meyer   b Wiltshire      10      not       out         27
K.Ibadulla         c Meyer   b Wells          20
S.Singh               lbw    b Cook           37
R.G.Carter         c Smith   b Cook            8
J.D.Bannister      c Wiltshire b Cook          1
W.E.Hollies           not       out            0
     Extras       (b 18, lb 6)                24    (lb 1)                    1
                                             ---                            ---
     TOTAL                                    373    (for 4 wkts)           119
```

```
WARWICKSHIRE    O    M    R    W     O    M    R    W      FALL OF WICKETS
Bannister       15   3    67   1     12   2    29   1         G    W    G    W
Carter          13   1    53   2     11   4    30   0        1st  1st  2nd  2nd
Townsend        8    3    15   0                        1st   81   38   45   18
Ibadulla        19   7    33   1     29   11   48   4   2nd   85  170   51   21
Hollies         25.5 4    62   6     43   18   66   3   3rd   86  170   89   63
Singh           12   1    38   0     20   6    41   2   4th  160  229   99   69
                                                       5th  185  239  103
GLOUCESTERSHIRE                                         6th  215  286  138
Smith           20   3    62   0                        7th  222  357  175
Wiltshire       13   1    50   2                        8th  240  367  193
Cook            41   13   86   5     13   3    30   0   9th  257  373  200
Wells           37   8    89   1     14   1    48   1   10th 270  373  221
Mortimore       13   3    35   0     11   0    28   2
Graveney        8    1    27   2
Emmett                               1    0    8    0
Nicholls                             0.1  0    4    0

Umpires: T.J.Bartley and W.Place
```

A couple of weeks later, Graveney made a career best 258 in the Test Match against the West Indies at Trent Bridge, but whereas Tom was supported by centuries from the two Peter's – May and Richardson – at Nottingham, he got little support from his Gloucestershire colleagues in this particular match in Birmingham in what became a virtuoso display of Graveney's wonderful batting talents.

Despite his fine efforts, it was not enough to win the game for his county. After Freddie Gardner had anchored the Warwickshire first innings with a patient 163, they only needed 118 to win on the final day. Gloucestershire immediately brought on their spinners, but Sam Cook, 'Bomber' Wells and John Mortimore could make little impression as Gardner again played watchfully to steer Warwickshire to a six-wicket victory.

ESSEX

1959 was a glorious summer from a meteorological point of view: it was nearly a glorious one for the Glosters too, as the West Country team made a sustained bid for the county title.

The season began with Tom Graveney taking over the captaincy from George Emmett, but a finger injury meant that Graveney spent much of the summer on the sidelines. Emmett was duly recalled, and together with Arthur Milton, shared the leadership duties as the county recorded a number of decisive victories in mid-season, including two wins over Northants, as well as beating Hampshire and Somerset.

In early August, the Gloucestershire side travelled to Leyton to meet Essex, knowing that another victory would provide a further boost to their title aspirations. The game was Ken Preston's Benefit Match, although an arm injury prevented the fast bowler from taking part in what proved to be a gripping contest.

Essex batted first and an unbeaten 177 from Doug Insole saw the home county to a sizeable first-innings score, with the Cambridge Blue pulling and driving strongly as his team declared on 364 for 6. Arthur Milton then played a captain's innings and continued in the rich vein of form that he had enjoyed for much of the summer, but when one short of his seventh century of the season he was caught off Barry Knight.

However, Milton's 99 had put the visitors within 35 of Essex's total and then for the second time in the match, Insole plundered some quick runs against the visiting bowlers before Essex declared again to leave Gloucestershire a tricky target of 212 in two hours and fifty minutes on the final afternoon.

With Surrey, the reigning Champions, losing at Worcester, and Yorkshire having already beaten Middlesex at Scarborough, the Gloucestershire batsmen knew another win was badly needed. However, they slumped dramatically to 131 for 8, and it looked as if they had squandered their chances. But Tony Brown, the twenty-three-year-old all-rounder, had other ideas, and he turned the

Arthur Miton

Tony Brown

```
                    ESSEX v GLOUCESTERSHIRE

Played at Leyton on 5th, 6th, 7th August 1959          Toss: Essex
Match Tied

                              ESSEX
L.A.Savill      c Brown    b Allen      25                    b Brown      10
G.Barker        c Mortimore b Brown      6
B.Taylor +      c Brown    b Allen      74 ( 4)              b Brown       6
D.J.Insole *      not        out       177 ( 5) c Cook      b Brown      90
T.E.Bailey      c Meyer    b Bernard    50 ( 6) c Milton    b Bernard    10
C.C.P.Williams             b Brown       3 ( 7) c Meyer     b Smith       1
J.Milner        c Milton   b Brown       6 ( 2) c Meyer     b Brown      11
B.R.Knight        not        out        17        c Meyer   b Smith       0
L.H.R.Ralph                                ( 3)             b Bernard    13
W.T.Greensmith                             ( 9)      not       out       28
A.Hurd
    Extras      (lb 5, nb 1)              6        (b 2, lb 2, nb 3)      7
                                        ---                             ---
    TOTAL              (for 6 wkts dec) 364        (for 8 wkts dec)     176

                         GLOUCESTERSHIRE
D.M.Young                  b Knight     14        c Ralph    b Bailey      0
C.A.Milton *    c Ralph    b Knight     99           run       out       23
R.B.Nicholls    c Taylor   b Hurd       64        c Milner   b Knight     41
J.B.Mortimore   c Taylor   b Hurd       30        c Williams b Ralph      12
D.Carpenter           c & b Greensmith   1                   b Greensmith 13
A.S.Brown                  b Knight     35        c Taylor   b Bailey     91
J.R.Bernard     c Insole   b Bailey      9 ( 8)              b Knight      1
D.A.Allen       c Bailey   b Greensmith 37 ( 9)      lbw     b Knight      5
D.R.Smith       c Williams b Knight      1 ( 7) c Taylor    b Greensmith  6
B.J.Meyer +     c Taylor   b Greensmith 21              not     out       13
C.Cook            not        out         0        c Milner   b Knight      0
    Extras      (b 3, lb 12, nb 3)      18        (lb 4, w 1, nb 1)        6
                                        ---                             ---
    TOTAL                              329                              211

GLOUCESTERSHIRE  O    M    R    W       O     M    R    W     FALL OF WICKETS
Smith           23    2   86    0      22     8   44    2          E    G    E    G
Brown           24    4   66    3      18.5   2   60    4         1st  1st  2nd  2nd
Milton           2    0   13    0                            1st   16   19   21    0
Cook            20   11   38    0       8     1   22    0    2nd  101  133   22   61
Mortimore       28    7   82    0                           3rd  114  199   31   73
Allen            8    4    6    2       6     0   20    0    4th  289  211   59   82
Bernard         13    1   67    1       8     1   23    2    5th  305  238   82  104
                                                            6th  325  263   83  110
ESSEX                                                       7th       267  109  111
Bailey          29    5   74    1      14     1   46    2    8th       276  176  131
Knight          25    4   69    4      17.4   2   64    4    9th       326       209
Ralph           23    6   56    0       7     1   30    1   10th       329       211
Greensmith      30.2  4   80    3       8     1   65    2
Hurd            18    6   32    2

Umpires: A.E.Fagg and T.W.Spencer
```

match on his head with a whirlwind assault, hitting 91 out of 127 in a shade over an hour and a half.

Brown had boldly struck 4 sixes and 10 fours, and with the equation now down to a handful of runs, the Essex captain, in a last throw of the dice, took the new ball. The target was reduced to a mere 3 runs when Trevor Bailey dismissed the youngster, leaving Gloucestershire's last pair of Barrie Meyer and Sam Cook at the wicket. Bailey then bowled a wide, before a single from Meyer brought the scores level, with Cook on strike to Bailey.

Cook had few aspirations as a batsman, but for once it looked as if he had struck the winning runs, as he flicked the ball off his legs. But Joe Milner took a stunning left-handed catch at short leg to leave the match tied.

SURREY

26, 27 August 1959 at Gloucester

After their thrilling tie at Leyton, the Gloucestershire side returned to winning ways at the Cheltenham Festival, thrashing Middlesex by an innings in Tom Graveney's Benefit Match, before beating Kent at Dover by 7 wickets.

Their next two games, against Yorkshire at Bristol and Surrey at Gloucester, were against their rivals at the top of the Championship table, and the home county's hopes were raised in the first encounter as Yorkshire were without their Test batsmen for the match at Nevil Road. Gloucestershire's morale was given another lift as Tom Graveney, now restored to fitness, struck a majestic 67, before a forthright 76 from John Mortimore allowed Graveney to declare on 294 and let his bowlers loose on the Tykes batting on a surface that had sweated under the covers.

In the space of seventy-five minutes, David Smith and Tony Brown dismissed the Yorkshire side for just 35, with Brown returning the remarkable figures of 7/11 from sixty-five unplayable deliveries. Brian Bolus was the only batsman to reach double figures, so when Yorkshire followed on, Bolus was promoted to open their innings. Once again, he was the only man to offer any resistance as the two Gloucestershire men dominated proceedings again, and despite a break for bad light, Gloucestershire wrapped up an innings victory after an hour's play on the final morning.

Their mood was high in the Gloucestershire camp as the players made their way to the Wagon Works for their vital game with Surrey. The home team knew they had to record another win if they were to maintain their title bid, and with the Gloucester wicket, as usual, favouring the slower bowlers, the game proved to be a classic encounter between Jim Laker and Tony Lock for Surrey, and Gloucestershire's David Allen, Sam Cook and John Mortimore.

The visitors won a decisive toss, and batted first, but within three-and-a-half hours, Allen and Cook had disposed of their much-vaunted line-up, for whom only John Edrich offered any lengthy resistance. But after three overs from the quicker bowlers, Laker and Lock were called up, and the two England men found conditions to their liking as the Gloucestershire batting crumbled. With the wicket never likely to get any better, Surrey had secured an invaluable lead of 29, but Sam Cook

David Allen

John Mortimore

```
                         GLOUCESTERSHIRE v SURREY

Played at Gloucester on 26th, 27th August 1959          Toss: Surrey
Surrey beat Gloucestershire by 89 runs
```

SURREY

J.H.Edrich		b Cook	45 (2)	c Milton	b Allen	14
A.B.D.Parsons	c Meyer	b Smith	7 (1)	c Milton	b Cook	0
K.F.Barrington	c Milton	b Smith	12 (4)	c Milton	b Cook	49
M.J.Stewart	lbw	b Allen	7 (5)	c Brown	b Mortimore	29
D.G.W.Fletcher	c Brown	b Allen	0 (6)		b Mortimore	0
R.Swetman +	c Smith	b Cook	13 (7)	c Brown	b Mortimore	11
D.Gibson	c Nicholls	b Allen	8 (3)		b Cook	0
E.A.Bedser	not	out	23	c Milton	b Cook	8
G.A.R.Lock	lbw	b Cook	1	c Young	b Cook	16
J.C.Laker	c Smith	b Allen	0	lbw	b Mortimore	3
A.V.Bedser *		b Allen	11	not	out	0
Extras	(lb 3)		3	(lb 1)		1
			---			---
TOTAL			130			131

GLOUCESTERSHIRE

D.M.Young	c Stewart	b Laker	8		b Laker	6
C.A.Milton	c Stewart	b Laker	12		b Lock	6
R.B.Nicholls	c A.V.Bedser	b Lock	2	c Stewart	b Laker	1
T.W.Graveney *		c & b Lock	31		b Lock	0
D.G.Hawkins	c Swetman	b Lock	0	st Swetman	b Laker	0
J.B.Mortimore	c Parsons	b Laker	13	c A.V.Bedser	b Lock	0
A.S.Brown		b Laker	0	c Lock	b Laker	5
D.A.Allen	c Lock	b Laker	16	not	out	18
D.R.Smith	c Barrington	b Lock	2	lbw	b Laker	28
B.J.Meyer +	c Edrich	b Lock	17	run	out	0
C.Cook	not	out	0	c Edrich	b Laker	0
Extras				(b 7)		7
			---			---
TOTAL			101			71

GLOUCESTERSHIRE	O	M	R	W	O	M	R	W
Smith	17	5	37	2				
Brown	3	1	5	0				
Mortimore	18	14	9	0	23	14	28	4
Allen	19.5	8	43	5	13	6	36	1
Cook	15	6	33	3	27.3	12	66	5

SURREY	O	M	R	W	O	M	R	W
A.V.Bedser	2	0	7	0				
Gibson	1	1	0	0				
Laker	21	7	53	5	15	6	27	6
Lock	23.2	13	32	5	15	6	37	3
E.A.Bedser	4	0	9	0				

FALL OF WICKETS	S	G	S	G
	1st	1st	2nd	2nd
1st	17	13	0	7
2nd	35	22	0	13
3rd	45	22	58	13
4th	45	32	77	13
5th	70	45	79	13
6th	93	45	102	22
7th	109	82	111	26
8th	110	82	111	66
9th	119	84	131	71
10th	130	101	131	71

```
Umpires: C.S.Elliott and D.Davies
```

then took two wickets with his first two deliveries as Surrey finished an eventful day 39 runs ahead with eight wickets standing.

Ken Barrington then played a little cameo on the second morning, hitting Cook for a huge six, and counter-attacking with glee. But Mortimore made inroads at the other end, and then after Cook had gained revenge by having Barrington caught by Milton for 49, the phlegmatic Cook finished off the Surrey resistance leaving Gloucestershire to chase 161 to maintain their title bid.

With the wicket dry and dusty, Alec Bedser opened the bowling with Laker and Lock. The Surrey 'spin twins' then enjoyed a field day as Gloucestershire slipped to 26 for 7, with none of their top order being able to make an impression on a wicket that had become a veritable minefield. A few lusty blows from David Allen and David Smith briefly hinted at something nearer parity, but with the ball misbehaving wickedly, it was only a matter of time before the Gloucestershire innings ended, and with it, all hopes of securing the county title disappeared.

South Africans

Having finished as Championship runners-up in 1959, much was expected of Gloucestershire in 1960. However, injuries hit Tom Graveney's team once again, and they were often unable to field their strongest team. But at the end of June, they gave a glimpse of their true form with a remarkable victory, achieved inside two days, against the touring South Africans.

This followed on from their 192-run victory over the 1959 Indians, but the defeat of the Springboks was far more emphatic, and achieved by a largely untried attack, with twenty-two-year-old Denis A'Court spearheading the Gloucestershire assault with a career best 6/25 in the tourists second innings.

The Bristol wicket was a very different one to the dry and sandy surfaces on which the county's spinners had posed problems for countless number of Test and county batsmen. This time it was well grassed, and with a green tinge and overcast skies, the conditions were perfect for the seam and swing bowlers – little surprise then that the contest was completed before tea on the second day.

After the tourists had batted first, David Smith made early inroads in the humid conditions, before John Mortimore in a steady spell of off-spin prevented the South Africans from gaining the upper hand, and although Hugh Tayfield opened his shoulders for a while, the visitors were dismissed for a modest 116.

But their efforts soon took on greater proportions as the Springbok's new bowlers reduced Gloucestershire to 9 for 4. Even worse was to follow as Arthur Milton, having bravely resisted for a while, fractured his right thumb after being hit by a sharply rising delivery. David Allen and David Smith made a few breezy hits, but wickets continued to fall as the tourists ended the day 43 runs ahead with 9 wickets in hand.

David Smith (back row, second from the left) with other members of the Gloucestershire team at Lord's in 1961. The other players are, from left to right, standing: D.G. A'Court, D.R. Smith, R.B. Nicholls, F.J. Andrew, D.A. Allen, D. Carpenter, B.J. Meyer. Sitting: J.B. Mortimore, D.M. Young, C.T.M. Pugh, C.A. Milton, D. Hawkins.

```
                    GLOUCESTERSHIRE v SOUTH AFRICANS

Played at Bristol on 29th, 30th June 1960            Toss: South Africans
Gloucestershire beat South Africans by 3 wickets
```

SOUTH AFRICANS

Batsman	1st innings		2nd innings	
T.L.Goddard *	b Smith	0	b A'Court	3
A.J.Pithey	b A'Court	8	c Meyer b Smith	5
S.O'Linn	b Smith	9	b Smith	0
C.A.R.Duckworth	b A'Court	17	b A'Court	4
J.H.B.Waite +	b Mortimore	20	b A'Court	4
P.R.Carlstein	c Graveney b Mortimore	1	lbw b A'Court	24
C.Wesley	c Graveney b Smith	7	b A'Court	1
H.J.Tayfield	c Hawkins b Mortimore	24	c Meyer b A'Court	3
J.E.Pothecary	c Pugh b Mortimore	13	b Smith	1
N.A.T.Adcock	c Smith b Mortimore	0	(11) b Smith	0
A.H.McKinnon	not out	16	(10) not out	0
Extras	(b 1)	1	(b 1, lb 3)	4
TOTAL		116		49

GLOUCESTERSHIRE

Batsman	1st innings		2nd innings	
D.M.Young	c Duckworth b Adcock	5	b Adcock	19
C.T.M.Pugh	b Adcock	2	c Waite b Adcock	0
T.W.Graveney *	lbw b Pothecary	1	(4) c Waite b Adcock	14
D.G.Hawkins	b Pothecary	0	(3) c Tayfield b Pothecary	1
C.A.Milton	retired hurt	16		
R.B.Nicholls	lbw b Goddard	10	(5) not out	35
D.A.Allen	c Waite b Goddard	23	(6) c Waite b Adcock	0
J.B.Mortimore	c Adcock b Tayfield	0	(7) b Goddard	2
D.R.Smith	st Waite b Tayfield	17	(8) c Goddard b Pothecary	6
B.J.Meyer +	b Tayfield	4	(9) not out	0
D.G.A'Court	not out	1		
Extras	(lb 2)	2	(b 6, lb 3, w 1)	10
TOTAL		81	(for 7 wkts)	87

GLOUCESTERSHIRE	O	M	R	W	O	M	R	W
A'Court	15	5	18	2	12	3	25	6
Smith	25	6	45	3	12	3	20	4
Mortimore	18.2	7	52	5				

SOUTH AFRICANS	O	M	R	W	O	M	R	W
Adcock	11	3	28	2	18	5	31	4
Pothecary	11	3	25	2	11.2	3	31	2
Goddard	10	7	6	2	7	3	15	1
Tayfield	9.4	2	20	3				

FALL OF WICKETS

	S	G	S	G
	1st	1st	2nd	2nd
1st	3	7	8	7
2nd	18	8	9	8
3rd	18	8	14	36
4th	55	9	18	37
5th	55	56	18	37
6th	61	59	26	40
7th	69	63	48	69
8th	89	78	49	
9th	97	81	49	
10th	116		49	

```
Umpires: A.E.Rhodes and R.S.Lay
```

The overhead conditions were still in the bowlers favour the following morning as the hostile David Smith, who was being tipped for England honours, and his young sidekick A'Court produced a remarkable spell that saw the tourists dismissed inside eighty-five minutes for just 49 – their lowest score against a county side since their 1912 tour.

The ball swung lavishly in the heavy atmosphere and with the inexperienced Court maintaining an accurate line outside off stump, the Springboks lost their wickets as they were time and again drawn into playing a shot, only to find the ball deviate away and find the outside edge of their bats. Only Phil Carlstein reached double figures as Gloucestershire were left needing 85 runs.

Neil Adcock then reduced the West Country side to 40 for 6 and with Milton unable to bat, it looked as if the tourists might win a remarkable game. But Ron Nicholls, the doughty batsman and professional footballer, calmly took the score to 64/6 when he had a stroke of good fortune as wicketkeeper John Waite spilled a chance behind the wicket. Spurred on by his reprieve, Nicholls remained defiant and the twenty-six year old played a gallant innings as the ball continued to fizz around, and a fierce square-cut off Pothecary settled the outcome and record a famous three-wicket win for Gloucestershire.

WARWICKSHIRE

While England was awash with World Cup football fever in 1966, Gloucestershire's cricketers produced two remarkable performances within the space of a fortnight in high summer. Firstly, they had a thrilling draw at Bristol in their tour match against the West Indians, after a fine first-innings century from Ron Nicholls, the thirty-two-year-old opening batsman. Gloucestershire's captain John Mortimore then challenged the tourists to make 285 in a shade over four hours on the final day, and with Joey Carew striking his first century of the tour, the visitors from the Caribbean looked like taking the honours.

Their victory charge was halted by Tony Brown, who dismissed Carew for 132, and after the fall of further wickets, the tourists entered the final over still needing 12 to win, with five wickets in hand. They got 11 off the first five balls, but David Holford was bowled by Brown's last ball attempting a mighty swish, and the contest was drawn with the scores level.

The following week Mortimore's men travelled to Edgbaston where once again Ron Nicholls played a fine innings. After both teams had made 251 in their first innings, Nicholls played beautifully on the placid Birmingham wicket, and with good support from the doughty Arthur Milton, they added 96 for the first wicket to give their side a good launch pad from which Mortimore was able to set Warwickshire a target of 193 in two hours.

Dennis Amiss and Mike Smith looked like making a mockery of Mortimore's challenge as the home team raced to 112 for 2 inside the first hour, but the Gloucestershire captain, together with

Ron Nicholls, John Mortimore and Arthur Milton.

```
                    WARWICKSHIRE v GLOUCESTERSHIRE

Played at Birmingham on 18th, 20th, 21st June 1966      Toss: Gloucestershire
Gloucestershire beat Warwickshire by 5 runs

                          GLOUCESTERSHIRE
R.B.Nicholls    c Cartwright b Webster     0     st A.C.Smith b Allan      69
C.A.Milton         lbw       b Cartwright 17     c Richardson b Jameson    52
D.W.J.Brown        lbw       b Allan      63     c Brown      b Allan      21
S.E.J.Russell   c Webster    b Barber     62
D.R.Shepherd    c Amiss      b Barber     10          not      out         13
D.A.Allen          not       out         45
J.B.Mortimore *              b Cartwright 37 ( 6)     not      out          1
A.S.Brown                    b Cartwright  2
A.R.Windows                  b Cartwright 11 ( 4) c M.J.K.Smith b Richardson 23
M.D.Mence
B.J.Meyer +
Extras          (b 1, lb 3)                4     (b 8, lb 5)               13
                                         ---                              ---
TOTAL                 (for 8 wkts dec)   251         (for 4 wkts dec)     192

                          WARWICKSHIRE
R.N.Abberley    c Milton    b Mortimore  56            run      out        11
R.W.Barber      c Shepherd  b Mortimore  56 ( 5) c Allen     b Mortimore   14
D.L.Amiss       c Allen     b Mortimore  45 ( 2) c Mence     b A.S.Brown   40
M.J.K.Smith *   c Mence     b Allen       4 ( 3) c Meyer     b Mortimore   56
J.A.Jameson     c D.W.J.Brown b Allen    16 ( 4)             b Allen       44
B.A.Richardson    lbw       b Allen      10 (10) c Windows   b Mortimore    5
T.W.Cartwright  c D.W.J.Brown b Allen     1     c Milton    b Mortimore    6
A.C.Smith +     c D.W.J.Brown b Allen    23             b Allen            2
R.V.Webster     c D.W.J.Brown b Mortimore 3 ( 6)            b Allen        0
J.M.Allan         not       out         10 (11)     not      out           6
D.J.Brown                   b Windows    19 ( 9)            b Allen        0
Extras          (b 4, lb 4)               8     (lb 3)                     3
                                         ---                              ---
TOTAL                                    251                              187

WARWICKSHIRE     O    M    R    W     O    M    R    W     FALL OF WICKETS
Brown            20   6    47   0     6    0    15   0       G    W    G    W
Webster          26   8    51   1     6    3    5    0      1st  1st  2nd  2nd
Cartwright      16.2  2    35   4     6    1    10   0  1st    3  107   96   43
Amiss            4    1    9    0                       2nd   25  114  135   54
Allan            31   12   58   1     23   4    75   2  3rd  126  123  164  132
Barber           17   5    47   2     11   2    28   0  4th  154  150  182  157
Jameson                               5    1    14   1  5th  155  171       160
Richardson                            12   1    32   1  6th  237  173       169
                                                       7th  239  199       172
GLOUCESTERSHIRE                                        8th  251  207       172
A.S.Brown        18   3    45   0     7    0    46   1  9th       222       176
Windows         12.5  2    39   1     5    0    40   0  10th      251       187
Mortimore        37   12   94   4    14.3  0    48   4
Allen            32   6    65   5     13   0    50   4

Umpires: J.Arnold and C.S.Elliott
```

David Allen, applied a brake on their progress. The pair of off-spinners had bowled well in Warwickshire's first innings as the Midlands county squandered an opening partnership of 107. Second time around, Mortimore and Allen tricked and teased the Warwickshire batsmen again and displayed the talents that brought them 9 and 39 caps respectively.

They were also aided by some fine fielding close to the wicket and safe catching in the outfield as the Warwickshire men tried to hit their way out of trouble. For the second time in the match, the jitters developed in the home batsmen, and in the final hour they collapsed against Gloucestershire's two spinners, and when the final wicket fell, Warwickshire were 6 runs short of their target.

ESSEX

Mike Procter was one of the finest new-ball bowlers on the county circuit in the early 1970's. The South African all-rounder was a fearsome sight charging towards the crease, with his blond hair flapping violently, as he delivered the ball chest-on, and almost off the wrong foot, with a whirlwind action. Even the most experienced and talented batsmen never found it easy facing him, and with his ability to gain lavish in-swing, as well as possessing a wickedly short bouncer, Procter could be relied upon to regularly mak an early breach in the visitor's side.

He was also a combative and classical batsman whose inspiring and savage strokes helped to win many games for his adopted county side, in addition to a place in the cricket record books in 1970/71 while playing for Rhodesia, as he struck six consecutive hundreds to emulate the feats of two other cricketing greats - C.B. Fry and Sir Don Bradman.

Mike Procter was therefore a true all-rounder, worth his place in any team – whether it be club or country – either as a batsman or a bowler, and someone who in either mode, with bat or ball, could produce a match-winning performance. This is precisely what he did in this classic match, as Procter helped Gloucestershire defeat Essex at Westcliff-on-Sea with a brilliant century and then a remarkable bowling spell during which he took a hat-trick of lbw's.

Mike Procter

The Gloucestershire squad of 1971. From left to right, back row: Graham Wiltshire, David Shepherd, Roger Knight, Jack Davey, Stuart Westley, Mike Bissex, John Sullivan, Sadiq Mohammad. Sitting: David Allen, David Smith, John Mortimore, Tony Brown (captain), Ron Nicholls, Barrie Meyer, Mike Procter.

In both innings, Procter arrived at the crease with his team struggling against the Essex seamers. In the first innings he counter-attacked with a forthright half-century and after David Shepherd had added some lusty blows of his own, Gloucestershire reached 184. They also secured a six-run lead as Procter and Brown subsequently shared seven Essex wickets between them as the home batsmen struggled against the lively Gloucestershire bowlers.

Procter then struck a magnificent century, despatching the Essex bowlers all around the pretty Chalkwell Park ground, and his furious assault demoralised their attack who, after their experiences the first time around, had fancied their chances of quickly dismissing the visitors. Sadiq Mohammad, the newly-signed Pakistani batsmen, lent stout support for a while, but it was largely through Procter's brilliance with the bat that Gloucestershire reached 238 to leave Essex needing 245 to win.

It was then Procter the destructive bowler who reduced Essex to 17 for 4, with the South African bowling around the wicket with fearsome accuracy and venom. In the space of twenty-seven balls, he took all four wickets at a cost of just 8 runs, with each batsman departing leg before. Edmeades, Ward and Boyce were dismissed in consecutive balls, as Procter became the first Gloucestershire player to take a hat-trick and score a century in a County Championship match.

'The wicket was still fairly lively and the ball swung a great deal,' Procter said after his record-breaking feat. 'I got Edmeades and Ward out in successive balls, and I conned Keith Boyce out for the hat-trick. I think he was expecting a bouncer first ball because he'd bowled a few at me in my

Procter in full flow.

innings. I pitched it well up and Keith was on the back foot, half expecting the bouncer and he was plumb lbw.'

The Springbok's hostility also saw Brian Taylor and Stuart Turner temporarily retire hurt, as Essex slipped into an even more desperate position. Despite a sober innings from Keith Fletcher, the home team never recovered after this new-ball blitz, as 'Proctershire' recorded a fine victory by 107 runs.

ESSEX v GLOUCESTERSHIRE

Played at Westcliff-on-Sea on 15th, 17th, 18th July 1972   Toss: Gloucestershire
Gloucestershire beat Essex by 107 runs

GLOUCESTERSHIRE

R.B.Nicholls	c Taylor	b Lever	8		lbw	b Boyce	9
J.C.Foat	c Turner	b Boyce	0	(7)	c Saville	b Acfield	6
R.D.V.Knight	c Turner	b Lever	16		run	out	10
M.J.Procter	c Taylor	b Turner	51		c Edmeades	b Turner	102
Sadiq Mohammad	c Taylor	b Lever	2	(2)	hit wicket	b Lever	48
D.R.Shepherd	c Saville	b Turner	59	(5)	lbw	b Acfield	4
M.Bissex	lbw	b Turner	0	(6)	c Taylor	b Acfield	9
A.S.Brown *		b Boyce	5		c Saville	b Boyce	4
R.Swetman +	c Taylor	b Lever	10		not	out	14
J.B.Mortimore	not	out	22		c East	b Turner	12
J.Davey		b Turner	4			b Lever	0
Extras	(b 1, lb 3, nb 3)		7		(b 5, lb 5, w 1, nb 9)		20
			---				---
TOTAL			184				238

ESSEX

B.E.A.Edmeades	c Procter	b Brown	72		lbw	b Procter	8
G.J.Saville	c Swetman	b Procter	1		lbw	b Procter	1
K.W.R.Fletcher	c Swetman	b Davey	20		c Bissex	b Davey	40
B.Ward	run	out	13		lbw	b Procter	0
K.D.Boyce	c Foat	b Brown	14		lbw	b Procter	0
B.Taylor *+	c Knight	b Procter	15			b Brown	37
S.Turner	c Shepherd	b Brown	17		c Swetman	b Knight	11
R.N.S.Hobbs		b Procter	4			b Procter	12
R.E.East	c Knight	b Brown	1		lbw	b Brown	19
J.K.Lever	not	out	9		c Nicholls	b Sadiq	1
D.L.Acfield	run	out	0		not	out	0
Extras	(b 3, lb 2, nb 7)		12		(b 1, w 5, nb 2)		8
			---				---
TOTAL			178				137

ESSEX	O	M	R	W	O	M	R	W
Boyce	21	3	59	2	27	8	59	2
Lever	16	3	39	4	17.4	2	60	2
Turner	21.3	4	67	4	23	5	45	2
Hobbs	4	1	12	0				
Acfield					15	2	54	3

GLOUCESTERSHIRE	O	M	R	W	O	M	R	W
Procter	15.4	4	43	3	16	4	30	5
Davey	15	2	70	1	11	0	38	1
Brown	22	6	53	4	16.2	6	36	2
Knight					6	2	14	1
Mortimore					1	0	5	0
Sadiq Mohammad					3	2	6	1

FALL OF WICKETS		G	E	G	E
		1st	1st	2nd	2nd
1st		3	16	25	10
2nd		17	57	55	17
3rd		28	81	94	17
4th		42	97	109	17
5th		98	123	135	51
6th		98	163	171	80
7th		113	164	192	89
8th		139	168	211	128
9th		174	177	236	137
10th		184	178	238	137

Umpires: W.L.Budd and A.G.T.Whitehead

SOMERSET

29, 31 May, 1 June 1976 at Taunton

There have been five occasions when Gloucestershire have won first-class matches after being asked to follow-on – three were at home in the nineteenth century in the years of Grace, another was in 1921 at the Spa Ground in Gloucester when Gloucestershire turned the tables on Essex, and the other – the most recent and the only one away from home – came at Taunton in 1976 during the county's derby match with neighbours Somerset over the May Bank Holiday.

This topsy-turvy match of changing luck and fortune began with Somerset making 333 for 7 in their 100 overs after batting first on a wicket with a greenish hue. Brian Rose batted superbly and countered the new ball menace of Jack Davey, Julian Shackleton and Mike Procter, before going on to a richly deserved century.

The overhead conditions were very different when Gloucestershire resumed on the Monday morning. The sky was overcast, with the remnants of an overnight storm, whilst a chill breeze blew across the ground, assisting the swing bowlers, and making batting an even more difficult proposition under the leaden skies. Ian Botham, the twenty-year-old all-rounder exploited the conditions perfectly, taking 6/25 as Gloucestershire were bustled out for 79.

With dampness still in the air, Brian Close, the Somerset skipper, opted to enforce the follow-on, even though he was without two of his bowlers – Graham Burgess was nursing a large swelling and a deep gash in an eyebrow after top-edging a sweep into his face on the first day, while Bob Clapp had sustained a side strain early in Gloucestershire's first innings.

Despite having limited resources, Close believed that his bowlers would exploit the conditions again. But Zaheer Abbas was in no mood to be subdued by either Botham or Keith Jennings, and the Pakistani made a superb 141 in two and three-quarter hours. Andy Stovold also made a pugnacious half-century and with useful support from David Shepherd and Julian Shackleton, Gloucestershire were able to clear the arrears and also secure a lead of 118.

Andy Stovold

David Shepherd

```
                    SOMERSET v GLOUCESTERSHIRE

Played at Taunton on 29th, 31st May, 1st June 1976        Toss: Somerset
Gloucestershire beat Somerset by 8 runs
```

SOMERSET

B.C.Rose	c Brassington b Graveney	104	c Shepherd	b Procter	48	
P.A.Slocombe	lbw	b Brown	36	lbw	b Brown	17
P.W.Denning		b Brown	41	c Sadiq	b Brown	4
D.B.Close *		b Brown	0	c Shackleton	b Brown	10
M.J.Kitchen	c Davey	b Graveney	69	c Shackleton	b Procter	10
D.J.S.Taylor +	not	out	41	c Sadiq	b Procter	0
G.I.Burgess	retired	hurt	10 (10)	not	out	1
I.T.Botham		b Graveney	13 (7)		b Procter	3
D.Breakwell		b Davey	0 (8)	c Shepherd	b Graveney	0
K.F.Jennings	not	out	3 (9)	c Stovold	b Procter	6
R.J.Clapp				c Sadiq	b Procter	1
Extras	(b 5, lb 9, nb 2)		16	(b 4, lb 5, nb 1)		10
TOTAL	(for 7 wkts)		333			110

GLOUCESTERSHIRE

Sadiq Mohammad	c Breakwell	b Botham	2	c & b Jennings		8
N.H.C.Cooper		b Botham	1		b Botham	38
Zaheer Abbas		b Clapp	5		b Close	141
M.J.Procter	c Taylor	b Botham	7	c Breakwell	b Close	32
A.W.Stovold	c Close	b Botham	18		b Botham	58
D.R.Shepherd		b Clapp	27	lbw	b Jennings	30
A.S.Brown *	lbw	b Botham	0		b Botham	4
D.A.Graveney	lbw	b Jennings	2		b Botham	0
J.H.Shackleton	c Close	b Clapp	0	st Taylor	b Breakwell	30
A.J.Brassington +	not	out	4	not	out	15
J.Davey		b Botham	1		b Botham	0
Extras	(b 4, lb 2, w 5, nb 1)		12	(b 8, lb 7, nb 1)		16
TOTAL			79			372

GLOUCESTERSHIRE	O	M	R	W	O	M	R	W
Davey	20	2	82	1	5	0	20	0
Shackleton	10	1	34	0				
Procter	16	5	32	0	14.3	4	35	6
Brown	28	8	64	3	9	2	27	3
Graveney	24	4	94	3	14	9	18	1
Sadiq Mohammad	2	0	11	0				
SOMERSET								
Clapp	13	6	18	3				
Botham	16.1	6	25	6	37.1	6	125	5
Jennings	8	1	24	1	25	6	71	2
Close	1	1	0	0	27	9	90	2
Kitchen	1	1	0	0	3	0	21	0
Rose					4	0	9	0
Breakwell					24	12	40	1

FALL OF WICKETS

	S	G	G	S
	1st	1st	2nd	2nd
1st	58	3	11	43
2nd	138	9	126	47
3rd	138	9	209	73
4th	237	29	236	97
5th	290	52	319	97
6th	326	52	325	100
7th	327	61	325	101
8th		68	327	108
9th		74	371	108
10th		79	372	110

Umpires: A.E.Fagg and H.Horton

With over four and a half hours left, and the skies having cleared, it seemed that Somerset's task would be a straightforward one, and with Rose in good form again against the Gloucestershire's new-ball bowlers, the Somerset openers had reached 43 before Tony Brown trapped Phil Slocombe leg before. He quickly followed up with the wickets of 'Dasher' Denning and Brian Close, as Somerset slipped to 73 for 3.

Even so, only 46 runs were still needed and Somerset were the firm favourites. However, Mike Procter then returned to the attack, and mixing pace with the occasional well flighted off-spinner, he completely changed the course of the game, with a spell of 6/13. Somerset's batsmen were completely mesmerised by the South African all-rounder, and they fell 8 runs short of their target to give Gloucestershire a remarkable victory.

WORCESTERSHIRE

27, 28, 29 July 1977 at Cheltenham

The daily grind of county cricket gradually left its mark on Mike Procter, especially on his right knee. The wear and tear meant that he cut down on his pace and slightly modified his bowling action, moving closer to the stumps. He also developed a ball that moved away from the batsman, thereby adding another weapon to his already impressive armoury. So rather than just flat-out bursts, he delivered longer spells of controlled medium-pace, and more frequent periods of off-spin.

Yet despite these aches and pains, Procter continued to produce some match-winning performances, and after being elevated to the captaincy in 1977, he led by example with both bat and ball. An example came in this next classic match in his first year in charge of the team, as Worcestershire visited the Cheltenham ground at the end of July, ten days or so after Gloucestershire had beaten Kent to win the Benson & Hedges Cup final at Lord's. Procter had been in awesome form as a bowler in this limited overs competition, and in the semi-final at Southampton, he had ripped out the heart of the Hampshire batting taking the first four wickets in five balls, including a hat-trick.

Despite the presence of New Zealander Glenn Turner and the experienced Basil D'Oliveira in their ranks, Worcestershire were bustled out by Procter in another fiery spell of new ball bowling at the College Ground, with the Springbok taking 7/35. The ball continued to move around when Gloucestershire batted, with Vanburn Holder, the West Indian paceman, finding conditions to his liking as Gloucestershire slipped to 43 for 3 before Alistair Hignell, the English rugby international, and the burly David Shepherd steadied the ship.

Mike proter hits a boundary batting against Middlesex.

```
                    GLOUCESTERSHIRE v WORCESTERSHIRE

Played at Cheltenham College on 27th, 28th, 29th July 1977      Toss: Worcestershire
Gloucestershire beat Worcestershire by an innings and 35 runs

                            WORCESTERSHIRE
G.M.Turner        c Zaheer     b Procter      9    c Procter    b Childs      16
J.A.Ormrod        c Stovold    b Brain       19 ( 7) c Hignell   b Graveney    44
P.A.Neale                      b Procter     38            lbw  b Procter      1
E.J.O.Hemsley     c Childs     b Procter     56                 b Procter     10
B.L.D'Oliveira    c Stovold    b Procter      0 ( 8) c Graveney  b Procter     23
S.P.Henderson     c Stovold    b Procter      2 ( 5)            b Procter      6
C.N.Boyns           lbw        b Procter      0 ( 6)      lbw   b Procter      1
D.J.Humphries +     lbw        b Brain       12 ( 2)      lbw   b Shackleton   0
V.A.Holder          run        out            8 (10)      lbw   b Procter     12
N.Gifford *       c Stovold    b Procter      9 ( 9)            b Graveney     8
J.Cumbes            not        out            0            not   out           2
    Extras        (lb 8, nb 6)              14       (b 9, nb 4)             13
                                            ---                             ---
    TOTAL                                   167                             136

                            GLOUCESTERSHIRE
Sadiq Mohammad    c Turner     b Holder       8
A.W.Stovold +     c Boyns      b Holder       0
Zaheer Abbas      c Humphries  b Holder      23
A.J.Hignell                    b Boyns       64
D.R.Shepherd      c Humphries  b Holder      38
J.H.Shackleton    c Turner     b Holder       0
M.J.Procter *     c   sub      b Cumbes     108
P.Bainbridge      c Humphries  b Holder      40
D.A.Graveney                   b Holder      32
B.M.Brain                      b Cumbes       6
J.H.Childs          not        out            0
    Extras        (b 2, lb 7, nb 10)         19
                                            ---
    TOTAL                                    338
```

GLOUCESTERSHIRE	O	M	R	W	O	M	R	W	FALL OF WICKETS			
										W	G	W
Brain	22	5	56	2						1st	1st	2nd
Procter	18.5	5	35	7	20	6	38	6	1st	16	1	2
Shackleton	11	1	27	0	6	1	6	1	2nd	61	19	10
Graveney	8	6	10	0	11.4	5	19	2	3rd	83	43	24
Childs	13	4	25	0	17	9	24	1	4th	83	108	30
Sadiq					11	4	36	0	5th	87	112	31
									6th	87	204	40
WORCESTERSHIRE									7th	114	259	104
Holder	35.5	7	117	7					8th	151	331	114
Cumbes	23	4	72	2					9th	163	338	134
Gifford	27	9	59	0					10th	167	338	136
Boyns	18	2	61	1								
Hemsley	3	0	10	0								

Umpires: W.L.Budd and W.E.Phillipson

After their resistance during Holder's second spell, Procter came in to apply the coup de grace, with a typically forthright century – his first of the summer – with the South African never failing to punish anything offline or short of a length. His hundred saw Gloucestershire to a first innings lead of 171, but when Worcestershire batted again, they might have wished they had a few more runs in the bank as Gloucestershire were without Brian Brain, their opening bowler.

However, Procter more than made up for the absence of his injured new-ball partner as Worcestershire slumped to 40 for 6, with Procter adding four more scalps to his tally. 'I didn't bowl very fast' he later said, 'because I knew I would have to do a lot of bowling. I kept hitting the seam, and it all worked out well.' Despite a stubborn 44 from Alan Ormrod, Worcestershire were bundled out again, to leave Gloucestershire celebrating an innings victory and Procter a match haul of thirteen wickets to go with his 108, in one of the finest all-round performances of the 1977 season.

SUSSEX

The second match of the 1977 Cheltenham Festival saw Sussex visit the College Ground to face Mike Procter's team who, after their recent successes in both versions of the game, were on the crest of a wave. With the county riding high in the Championship table, there was plenty of talk around the Cotswolds town of the county becoming County Champions.

However, the visitors had a very useful and experienced attack, and after the way the ball had moved around in the previous match against Worcestershire, it seemed as if the conditions might suit Sussex's new-ball pairing of John Snow, the former England pace bowler, plus Imran Khan, the great Pakistani all-rounder.

But Gloucestershire held a trump card of their own – the magnificent artistry of batsman Zaheer Abbas, who with razor-sharp reflexes, supple wrists and a wonderful eye, was among the finest batsmen in the world at that time. The modest and quietly spoken Pakistani belied his mild disposition off the field by ruthlessly and mercilessly dominating all manner of bowling – fast, slow, left arm and right – and as he proved on many occasions during the 1970s he more than lived up to being called the 'Asian Bradman'.

On this particular occasion, he carved his own niche in the record books as, for the third time in his illustrious career, Zaheer struck a double and single century in the same match. He became the first man in cricket history to achieve this feat three times, and he added a fourth at Bath in 1981 against Somerset.

Despite the presence of Snow and Imran, the Sussex bowlers were put to the sword by the Pakistani, as time and again his imperious drives through the covers pierced the arc of fielders who were left exchanging helpless glances as the ball sped down the slope to the boundary boards. 'Zed' followed his first innings 205* with an equally exquisite 108* in the second innings, and one of the

Zaheer Abbas

```
                        GLOUCESTERSHIRE v SUSSEX

Played at Cheltenham College on 30th July, 1st, 2nd August 1977        Toss: Sussex
Gloucestershire beat Sussex by 8 wickets

                                  SUSSEX
J.R.T.Barclay     st Stovold  b Childs      105   c Bainbridge b Procter    11
P.J.Graves *      c Stovold   b Procter      56                b Graveney   11
R.D.V.Knight                  b Graveney     18              c & b Graveney 21
Javed Miandad     c Procter   b Graveney     48   c Stovold   b Graveney    30
Imran Khan                    b Graveney      1               run out       39
P.W.G.Parker      c Zaheer    b Graveney     32   c Hignell   b Graveney     2
M.A.Buss          st Stovold  b Childs        9               lbw  b Procter 30
A.Long +          not         out        11 ( 9)              b Procter     20
J.A.Snow          not         out         8 ( 8)              b Childs      56
J.Spencer                                                     not  out       9
R.G.L.Cheatle                                     c Shackleton b Childs      8
   Extras         (b 4, lb 14, w 1, nb 2)   21    (b 17, lb 2, nb 6)        25
                                            ---                            ---
   TOTAL                      (for 7 wkts)  309                            262

                              GLOUCESTERSHIRE
Sadiq Mohammad    c Barclay   b Imran         0   c Barclay   b Javed       33
A.W.Stovold +                c & b Buss       61   c Long      b Imran       30
Zaheer Abbas      not         out           205               not  out     108
A.J.Hignell       c Long      b Cheatle       8               not  out      33
M.J.Procter *                 b Imran         17
D.R.Shepherd      c Knight    b Spencer       32
P.Bainbridge      c Javed     b Buss           7
D.A.Graveney      c Long      b Snow          16
J.H.Shackleton    not         out             1
M.J.Vernon
J.H.Childs
   Extras         (lb 2, w 1, nb 3)           6   (b 5, lb 4, w 3, nb 3)    15
                                             ---                           ---
   TOTAL                      (for 7 wkts)   353              (for 2 wkts)  219
```

GLOUCESTERSHIRE	O	M	R	W	O	M	R	W		FALL OF WICKETS			
										S	G	S	G
Procter	25	7	51	1	29	5	91	3		1st	1st	2nd	2nd
Vernon	7	1	37	0	2	0	13	0	1st	119	2	12	47
Shackleton	12	1	38	0	3	0	22	0	2nd	144	146	47	106
Childs	23	4	72	2	13.4	7	25	2	3rd	222	169	51	
Graveney	33	5	90	4	35	10	84	4	4th	224	200	93	
Sadiq Mohammad					1	0	2	0	5th	266	300	99	
									6th	284	319	144	
SUSSEX									7th	291	349	174	
Imran Khan	17	5	52	2	7	3	15	1	8th		214		
Snow	18	3	68	1	3	0	11	0	9th		248		
Spencer	16	2	58	1					10th		262		
Buss	24	5	53	2	4	0	16	0					
Cheatle	18	3	79	1	18	3	71	0					
Barclay	2	1	3	0	10	1	45	0					
Javed Miandad	1	0	12	0	7.4	0	44	1					
Knight	4	0	22	0									
Long					1	0	2	0					

Umpires: W.L.Budd and D.O.Oslear

Sussex fielders was so driven to exasperation that he wailed to a colleague 'We won't get this bloody bloke out if we wait until Cheltenham next year!'

Thanks to his wonderful batting, Gloucestershire reached their target of 219 inside four hours and as the early evening shadows set on the historic college ground, Gloucestershire's supporters were able to toast the performances of 'Zed' for maintaining their Championship quest. Further victories over Hampshire and Glamorgan kept them in the hunt, but in their vital match against Hampshire at the end of the summer, Zaheer was handicapped by a thigh strain, and without the experience of injured seamers Jack Davey and Tony Brown, Gloucestershire went down by six wickets to finish up five points behind Middlesex and Kent in third place.

INDIANS

A few cynics had claimed that 'Proctershire' relied heavily on their overseas men, but while this victory over the 1979 Indians saw another remarkable bowling performance from their inspirational captain, it only came about as a result of two handsome efforts from two of Gloucestershire's younger brigade of England-qualified cricketers – the twenty-one-year-old all-rounder Phil Bainbridge and David Partridge, the twenty-four-year-old left-hander from Birdlip – who mounted a valiant fightback with their team in danger of following on after the tourists had cruised to 337 for 5 on the opening day.

A characteristically sublime century from Sunil Gavaskar gave the tourists a good launch pad, and his stand of 160 in two hours and twenty minutes for the second wicket appeared to have put the Indians into a dominant position, especially as Gloucestershire slipped to 91 for 6 in reply.

It looked as if the tourists would record another comprehensive victory over county opposition, but Bainbridge and Partridge then belied their inexperience and more than doubled the score, with the phlegmatic Bainbridge unfurling some assertive strokes off the back foot, and in particular a firm whip through midwicket. His stand with the equally stubborn Partridge was worth 116 runs when the latter fell to Venkat, but Bainbridge remained resolute and appeared to be on course for a maiden first-class century.

But Procter had noticed how the morale of the Indians had dropped, and now that the follow-on had been avoided, the Indians would have to bat again. Everyone expected the Gloucestershire lower order to see out the day under the overcast conditions, but Procter decided to declare shortly before the close.

It proved a masterstroke as the tourists, perhaps surprised by Procter's decision, lost three quick wickets as they juggled their batting order, thinking that they might give others a chance for batting practice. There was a thick cloud cover the following morning when the Indians resumed on 14 for 3, and having regained the initiative the previous night, Procter was determined not to let the tourists off the hook. While not at full pace, the South

Phil Bainbridge

GLOUCESTERSHIRE v INDIANS

Played at Bristol on 21st, 22nd, 23rd July 1979   Toss: Indians
Gloucestershire beat Indians by 7 wickets

INDIANS

S.M.Gavaskar	c Bainbridge b Childs	116 (7)	c Brassington b Procter 30
C.P.S.Chauhan	c Sadiq b Brain	12 (1)	b Brain 4
D.B.Vengsarkar	b Brain	96 (6)	c Sadiq b Procter 0
A.D.Gaekwad	b Bainbridge	23 (2)	b Brain 0
Yashpal Sharma	not out	64	c Zaheer b Procter 33
B.P.Patel	c Sadiq b Bainbridge	12 (4)	c Sadiq b Procter 4
Yajurvindra Singh	not out	2 (3)	lbw b Procter 1
K.D.Ghavri			b Brain 22
S.Venkataraghavan *			b Procter 10
B.Reddy +			not out 4
B.S.Chandrasekhar			b Procter 0
Extras	(b 2, lb 5, nb 5)	12	(b 2, lb 3, w 2, nb 2) 9
TOTAL	(for 5 wkts dec)	337	117

GLOUCESTERSHIRE

A.W.Stovold	c Vengsarkar b Ghavri	0	c Sharma b Venkat 45
Sadiq Mohammad	lbw b Singh	0	b Ghavri 35
Zaheer Abbas	b Singh	59	not out 53
A.J.Hignell	b Singh	9	c Sharma b Singh 32
A.J.Brassington +	b Singh	0	
M.J.Procter *	c sub b Singh	17 (5)	not out 24
P.Bainbridge	not out	81	
M.D.Partridge	c Gavaskar b Venkat	65	
D.A.Graveney	not out	13	
R.M.Brain			
J.H.Childs			
Extras	(lb 4, w 1, nb 5)	10	(b 4, lb 4, w 1, nb 5) 14
TOTAL	(for 7 wkts dec)	254	(for 3 wkts) 203

GLOUCESTERSHIRE	O	M	R	W	O	M	R	W
Brain	18	2	44	2	17	3	56	3
Procter	12	4	28	0	15.3	8	13	7
Partridge	20	2	105	0	6	1	22	0
Bainbridge	13	4	39	2	5	0	17	0
Childs	18	1	72	1				
Graveney	8	1	37	0				
INDIANS								
Ghavri	17	5	70	1	12	2	47	1
Singh	21	6	75	5	10	1	47	1
Chandrasekhar	17	4	56	0	7	1	33	0
Venkataraghavan	12	2	38	1	19	4	48	1
Chauhan	1	0	5	0	2	0	14	0

FALL OF WICKETS

	I 1st	G 1st	I 2nd	G 2nd
1st	47	0	6	65
2nd	207	0	7	95
3rd	235	33	10	174
4th	274	40	14	
5th	314	88	22	
6th		91	56	
7th		207	96	
8th			110	
9th			117	
10th			117	

Umpires: D.J.Constant and J.G.Langridge

African bowled a testing line and length, and even though Gavaskar, batting at number seven, stoutly defended, the damage had been done, as Procter made further inroads to finish with 7/13.

Gloucestershire's target was 201 and with Andy Stovold and Sadiq Mohammad providing a firm base, Gloucestershire eased to a seven-wicket victory. There were still 17 overs of the final 20 to spare, when Procter finished the game with two sixes off Chetan Chauhan.

LEICESTERSHIRE

Ten days after beating the 1979 Indians, Gloucestershire recorded another handsome victory, with their influential captain producing yet again, a superb all-round performance as Leicestershire were beaten at Bristol by eight wickets.

Gloucestershire had enjoyed little success at their headquarters, having not won a Championship game at Nevil Road for almost three years. When Leicestershire batted first, there seemed little to suggest that this pattern would be changed as consistent batting by their top order saw the visitors to 314 for 4. The small and stocky Sadiq Mohammad then launched the Gloucestershire reply with a series of powerful cuts and pulls, as well as some clever dabs behind square. But he lost three quick partners as Gloucestershire slipped to 25 for 3, before the close thanks to a fine new-ball burst by Ken Higgs.

The following morning they recovered thanks to a furious counter-attack from their captain who in the space of 104 minutes smashed 122 with two sixes and nineteen rasping fours. He raced to a century before lunch before being caught behind off Gordon Parsons after adding 167 for the fifth wicket with Sadiq (right).

The dapper Pakistani then found a useful ally in David Partridge, boosted by his fine performance against the Indians. With Partridge settling in at the other end, Sadiq duly reached his century, and after adding a further 99 runs, he was caught and bowled by John Steele before Partridge astutely marshalled the tail to further extend Gloucestershire's lead to 74.

Leicestershire lost two wickets in clearing the arrears, but then a heavy shower caused an interruption and when play resumed, Procter was lethal on the damp surface. In the space of sixteen balls, he scythed through the visitors' middle order, taking five wickets at a cost of just 1 run, and in the process claimed another hat-trick, dismissing Chris Balderstone, Paddy Clift and Ken Shuttleworth in consecutive deliveries. By the time Gloucestershire batted again, the wicket had dried out, and they eased to an eight-wicket win.

GLOUCESTERSHIRE v LEICESTERSHIRE

Played at Bristol on 1st, 2nd, 3rd August 1979   Toss: Leicestershire
Gloucestershire beat Leicestershire by 8 wickets

LEICESTERSHIRE

B.Dudleston	lbw	b Bainbridge	78	c Childs		b Bainbridge	12
J.F.Steele		b Brain	4			b Procter	7
J.C.Balderstone	c Stovold	b Graveney	95	c Hignell		b Procter	56
B.F.Davison	c Brassington	b Childs	41		lbw	b Procter	35
N.E.Briers	not	out	66 (6)			b Brain	3
R.W.Tolchard +	not	out	21 (7)		not	out	9
N.G.B.Cook			(5)	c Sadiq		b Brain	8
P.B.Clift					lbw	b Procter	0
K.Shuttleworth					lbw	b Procter	0
G.J.Parsons				c Hignell		b Procter	0
K.Higgs *				c Brassington		b Procter	1
Extras	(lb 3, nb 6)		9	(lb 1, w 1, nb 1)			3
TOTAL	(for 4 wkts)		314				134

GLOUCESTERSHIRE

A.W.Stovold		b Higgs	4			b Cook	25
Sadiq Mohammad	c &	b Steele	137		not	out	28
Zaheer Abbas	c Tolchard	b Higgs	8		run	out	8
A.J.Hignell	lbw	b Higgs	0		not	out	0
P.Bainbridge	c Briers	b Cook	14				
M.J.Procter *	c Tolchard	b Parsons	122				
M.D.Partridge	not	out	74				
D.A.Graveney	c &	b Steele	1				
B.M.Brain		b Parsons	9				
A.J.Brassington +	not	out	7				
J.H.Childs							
Extras	(b 7, lb 3, nb 2)		12				
TOTAL	(for 8 wkts)		388	(for 2 wkts)			61

GLOUCESTERSHIRE	O	M	R	W	O	M	R	W
Brain	17	3	55	1	15	4	33	2
Procter	8	2	32	0	17.5	5	26	7
Partridge	14	4	44	0	4	0	13	0
Childs	24	5	97	1	5	0	23	0
Graveney	27	13	55	1	7	1	17	0
Bainbridge	10	5	22	1	5	4	3	1
Sadiq Mohammad					6	1	16	0

LEICESTERSHIRE	O	M	R	W	O	M	R	W
Parsons	14	3	77	2				
Higgs	19	4	58	3	3	2	9	0
Shuttleworth	16	3	56	0	4	2	7	0
Cook	24	8	59	1	8	2	15	1
Steele	11	2	48	2	2.4	0	7	0
Clift	14	3	62	0	7	1	23	0
Balderstone	2	1	16	0				

FALL OF WICKETS				
	L	G	L	G
	1st	1st	2nd	2nd
1st	7	15	8	37
2nd	160	25	25	60
3rd	202	25	95	
4th	231	64	113	
5th		231	123	
6th		330	124	
7th		336	124	
8th		354	124	
9th			132	
10th			134	

Umpires: R.Julian and R.Palmer

DERBYSHIRE

1, 3, 4 June 1985 at Derby

After several indifferent seasons, Gloucestershire carefully rebuilt their side during the mid 1980s, signing some experienced players from other counties, and hiring another quality overseas player in Courtney Walsh. The tall and languid West Indian joined the county's staff in 1984, and the following summer he made an immediate impact taking 85 wickets as well as forging a potent and at times frightening bowling partnership with David Lawrence, the twenty-one-year-old tearaway, born in Gloucester of Jamaican parents.

The wickets at Bristol, so long a dry and dusty haven for the county's spinners, now had a more verdant tint, but as this classic match at Derby proved, it was not just at Bristol where the Gloucestershire quick bowlers prospered, as the two pacemen shared the ten wickets between them as Derbyshire, chasing 309 were fired out for just 82 inside 24 overs.

Their hostile performance was even more surprising given the fact that until Derbyshire's second innings the batsmen had dominated proceedings, with over 1,000 runs being scored for the loss of only twelve wickets. Indeed, on the opening day, the Gloucestershire batsmen had set the tone by making 398 for 3 with Phil Bainbridge and Bill Athey sharing a stand of 305 for the fourth wicket.

Athey had been another shrewd acquisition by the West Country side in 1984, and in the course of the next nine years, the gritty Yorkshireman brought a touch of steel to the county's upper order.

David Graveney – Gloucestershire's captain in 1985.

```
                        DERBYSHIRE v GLOUCESTERSHIRE

Played at Derby on 1st, 3rd, 4th June 1985          Toss: Derbyshire
Gloucestershire beat Derbyshire by 226 runs

                            GLOUCESTERSHIRE
A.W.Stovold              b Warner      20    st Maher    b Barnett    112
P.W.Romaines    c Roberts b Finney     32    c Mortensen b Holding      5
C.W.J.Athey          c & b Barnett    170    st Maher    b Barnett     58
P.Bainbridge       not        out     151 ( 5)   not        out        36
B.F.Davison        not        out      15 ( 4) c Roberts  b Barnett    47
K.M.Curran                                       not        out        14
J.W.Lloyds
D.A.Graveney *
R.C.Russell +
D.V.Lawrence
C.A.Walsh
    Extras      (lb 7, nb 3)           10    (b 3, lb 10, w 1, nb 5)    19
                                      ---                             ---
    TOTAL          (for 3 wkts dec)   398       (for 4 wkts dec)      291

                              DERBYSHIRE
B.J.M.Maher +   c Stovold b Graveney   46 ( 2) c Russell  b Walsh       1
A.Hill            retired    hurt       9 (10)    not        out       10
K.J.Barnett *            b Lloyds      83 ( 1)    lbw      b Walsh      19
J.E.Morris      c Stovold b Lloyds     22 ( 3) c Russell  b Lawrence    5
B.Roberts          not        out     100 ( 4) c Davison  b Lawrence    2
W.P.Fowler         lbw      b Walsh     13 ( 5) c Lloyds   b Walsh       0
R.J.Finney      c Romaines b Graveney   82              b Lawrence      1
G.Miller           not        out       1 ( 6)    lbw     b Lawrence   11
A.E.Warner                                                b Walsh      12
M.A.Holding                             ( 8) c Bainbridge b Lawrence   13
O.H.Mortensen                                    lbw      b Walsh       0
    Extras      (b 6, lb 4, w 1, nb 14) 25       (w 2, nb 6)            8
                                      ---                             ---
    TOTAL          (for 5 wkts dec)   381                              82
```

DERBYSHIRE	O	M	R	W	O	M	R	W		FALL OF WICKETS			
Holding	17	4	59	0	7	0	33	1		G	D	G	D
Mortensen	17	3	68	0	11	4	29	0		1st	1st	2nd	2nd
Warner	19	4	75	1	10	2	34	0	1st	30	135	10	7
Finney	22	2	86	1	9	0	44	0	2nd	65	177	157	22
Miller	2	0	7	0	21	4	54	0	3rd	370	178	235	28
Roberts	4	0	27	0					4th		206	236	28
Barnett	19	2	69	1	28	4	84	3	5th		375		28
									6th				34
GLOUCESTERSHIRE									7th				53
Lawrence	13.2	1	70	0	12	1	38	5	8th				59
Walsh	23	2	84	1	12	2	44	5	9th				82
Graveney	34	8	94	2					10th				82
Curran	7	0	42	0									
Lloyds	15	2	75	2									
Athey	1	0	6	0									

```
Umpires: B.Leadbeater and R.A.White
```

As befitted someone with experience at Test level and in one-day internationals, Athey was a fluent and accomplished stroke-maker, and together with Bainbridge, their partnership ended just 31 runs of the club's all-time record.

Both passed a thousand Championship runs and finished in first and second place in the county's averages, as Gloucestershire side ended the summer in third place. Between them, Athey and Bainbridge scored over 2,700 runs in Championship matches, and with Walsh and Lawrence sharing 161 wickets between them, Gloucestershire emerged from the doldrums to record seven wins in the competition.

WARWICKSHIRE

For much of the 1985 season, the rejuvenated Gloucestershire side looked capable of winning the county title for the first time since 1877, and their pursuit of the Championship pennant only ended late in the season when some of the batsmen lost form and the weather gods turned against them.

But in this classic match at the Cheltenham Festival everything went in their favour, and when rain washed out play in other parts of the country, the sun was shining in the Cotswolds as Gloucestershire recorded a seven-wicket win to go back to the top of the table.

On one of the fastest ever wickets prepared at the historic college ground, the first day saw twenty wickets fall, as firstly, Walsh and Lawrence brushed aside the Warwickshire batting in just two and a half hours, with Walsh generating fearsome pace and bounce from the Cheltenham wicket to return figures of 7/51.

But the home team were soon in trouble slipping to 19 for 4 as Gladstone Small, another English bowler with Caribbean roots, made early inroads. He received useful support from Paul Smith, but they did not have either the class or stamina of the Gloucestershire attack, and it was left to two other shrewd acquisitions – the Zimbabwean Kevin Curran and the former Somerset all-rounder Jeremy Lloyds to oversee a recovery that saw an invaluable 133 runs being added for the fifth wicket as Gloucestershire secured a first-innings lead of 126 runs.

However, rain then swept in on the second day, and resulted in the loss of almost the entire day's play. When play resumed under gun-metal grey skies, a draw seemed the likely outcome, but Walsh then produced another explosive spell, and despite some brave resistance

Courtney Walsh

```
                    GLOUCESTERSHIRE v WARWICKSHIRE

Played at Cheltenham College on 17th, 19th, 20th August 1985      Toss: Warwickshire
Gloucestershire beat Warwickshire by 7 wickets

                              WARWICKSHIRE
R.I.H.B.Dyer      c Russell    b Walsh        9    c Lloyds    b Walsh      10
G.J.Lord          c Athey      b Lawrence     0    c Lloyds    b Walsh      18
A.I.Kallicharran  c Lawrence   b Walsh       34    c Russell   b Curran     20
D.L.Amiss         c Athey      b Lawrence    14    c Stovold   b Lawrence   45
G.W.Humpage +     c Russell    b Lawrence     0    c Russell   b Walsh      45
P.A.Smith         c Russell    b Walsh       38    c Russell   b Walsh       8
A.M.Ferreira      c Russell    b Walsh        4      not         out        34
D.A.Thorne        c Graveney   b Walsh        0    c Russell   b Walsh       0
G.C.Small              not        out         7    c Athey     b Walsh      10
A.R.K.Pierson                  b Walsh        2                b Lawrence    3
N.Gifford *                    b Walsh        4    c Athey     b Lawrence    0
    Extras       (b 4, lb 10, nb 1)          15    (lb 2, w 7, nb 9)        18
                                             ---                           ---
         TOTAL                               127                           211

                              GLOUCESTERSHIRE
A.W.Stovold       c Pierson    b Smith        6                b Ferreira   10
A.J.Wright                     b Small        7    c Gifford   b Small       7
C.W.J.Athey       c Humpage    b Smith        0      not         out        18
B.F.Davison       c Ferreira   b Small        0
J.W.Lloyds        c Humpage    b Ferreira    54      not         out        23
K.M.Curran                     b Small       63 ( 4)  lbw       b Ferreira   10
I.R.Payne         c Humpage    b Ferreira    11
R.C.Russell +     c Humpage    b Small       17
D.A.Graveney *         not        out        29
D.V.Lawrence                   b Small        9
C.A.Walsh                      b Ferreira    31
    Extras      (b 1, lb 7, w 1, nb 17)      26    (b 5, lb 8, w 5)         18
                                             ---                           ---
         TOTAL                               253    (for 3 wkts)            86
```

GLOUCESTERSHIRE	O	M	R	W	O	M	R	W	FALL OF WICKETS			
										W	G	W	G
Lawrence	11	2	34	3	24.2	2	95	3		1st	1st	2nd	2nd
Walsh	15.5	3	51	7	24	6	77	6	1st	9	17	29	18
Curran	5	0	28	0	5	2	30	1	2nd	15	17	32	19
Payne					2	0	7	0	3rd	42	17	80	48
									4th	46	19	151	
WARWICKSHIRE									5th	99	152	155	
Small	21	3	80	5	9	4	20	1	6th	104	152	166	
Smith	11	1	80	2	1	0	12	0	7th	104	169	166	
Ferreira	22	1	85	3	9	0	27	2	8th	121	192	186	
Gifford					1	0	14	0	9th	123	206	201	
									10th	127	253	211	

```
Umpires: C.Cook and J.H.Harris
```

from the experienced Dennis Amiss, and wicketkeeper Geoff Humpage, the Jamaican's ferocious bowling proved too much for the Warwickshire batsmen.

With clever changes in both pace and length, he steadily worked his way through the opposition, and supported by some fine catching in the slips, as well as from Jack Russell behind the stumps, Walsh added a further six wickets to take his match analysis to 13/128.

SUSSEX

Mark Alleyne has been at the helm in the last few years as Gloucestershire have enjoyed one of their finest periods in their history, particularly in the one-day competitions. Few could have forecast such a glittering period of success when Alleyne first joined the county's staff in the mid-1980s, but Gloucestershire's coaching staff knew they had made a shrewd acquisition, as what set Alleyne apart from the other enthusiastic colts was a steely keen competitive streak and a single-minded purpose; virtues that were clearly in evident in this next classic match, as Alleyne became the county's youngest ever centurion.

The first day had ended with the eighteen-year-old Alleyne, in only his eighth first-class innings, unbeaten on 99, after calmly defying the Sussex attack throughout the afternoon and early evening. But the youngster was not overawed by their reputation, and on the

Mark Alleyne

second morning, he gave further evidence of his rock-solid temperament by calmly scoring the single he needed for his maiden first-class century. His sterling efforts were given extra value as Sussex's batsmen then struggled against the pace of David Lawrence, who took three wickets in four balls, supported by the clever spin of David Graveney, who claimed four wickets as Sussex were forced to follow-on 248 runs in arrears.

Batting for a second time, it was the classy speed of Walsh who made the early incision but the Sussex middle order fought back as Gloucestershire were handicapped by a leg injury to David Lawrence. Although Walsh remained a handful, batting was a slightly easier proposition than in the first innings. Paul Parker duly made a spirited century and received good support from the all-rounders Imran Khan and Colin Wells. Both fell to Jeremy Lloyds, and the off-spinner then worked his way through the remaining batting as Sussex ended up just 93 runs ahead.

Despite their slender lead, the visitors were not going to go down without a fight, and slipped to 31 for 6 against some lively bowling from Imran Khan and Andy Babington, who later played for Gloucestershire. On this particular day, he took a hat-trick, after dismissing Bainbridge, Curran and Lloyds and the record books started to be thumbed through in search of the last time a county side had won after being invited to follow-on. But Alleyne calmly settled the Gloucestershire nerves, and together with Jack Russell, they took the home team closer to their target, before Alleyne was adjudged leg before to Dermot Reeve. Imran Khan then grabbed two quick wickets to leave Gloucestershire on 82 for 9.

```
                        GLOUCESTERSHIRE v SUSSEX

Played at Bristol on 16th, 17th, 18th July 1986        Toss: Sussex
Gloucestershire beat Sussex by 1 wicket

                            GLOUCESTERSHIRE
A.J.Wright              b Imran        46                b Imran         0
A.W.Stovold            b Imran        62    c Parker     b Babington     6
K.P.Tomlins     c Green b Mays        51                b Imran        13
P.Bainbridge           b Imran         1                b Babington     5
K.M.Curran             b Mays          0    c Gould      b Babington     0
J.W.Lloyds      c Imran b Mays        17    c Green      b Babington     0
M.W.Alleyne      not          out    116    lbw          b Reeve        19
R.C.Russell +    not          out     45    not          out           23
C.A.Walsh                                   lbw          b Imran         0
D.A.Graveney *                              c Gould      b Imran        10
D.V.Lawrence                                not          out            7
    Extras      (b 1, lb 7, w 1, nb 3)  12  (b 2, lb 3, w 4, nb 2)     11
                                       ---                             ---
    TOTAL          (for 6 wkts dec)   350        (for 9 wkts)          94

                                SUSSEX
D.K.Standing            b Lawrence     16                b Walsh         9
A.M.Green      c Russell b Lawrence     0                b Walsh        35
P.W.G.Parker           b Lawrence      0                b Walsh       120
Imran Khan     c Russell b Lawrence     0    st Russell  b Lloyds       47
C.M.Wells      c Graveney b Walsh      13    c Russell   b Lloyds       50
A.P.Wells      c Stovold b Graveney    19    c Stovold   b Lloyds        0
D.A.Reeve      c Wright  b Walsh       27                b Lloyds       31
I.J.Gould *+   c Wright  b Graveney     2    lbw         b Lloyds        5
A.C.S.Pigott   c Bainbridge b Graveney  3                b Walsh        17
C.S.Mays         not          out       8                b Graveney      4
A.M.Babington          b Graveney       1    not         out            0
    Extras        (lb 5, nb 8)         13    (b 5, lb 5, w 5, nb 8)     23
                                      ---                              ---
    TOTAL                             102                              341
```

```
SUSSEX        O    M    R    W     O    M    R    W    FALL OF WICKETS
Imran        28.4 10   59    3    18    7   42    4         G    S    S    G
Pigott       15    5   37    0                           1st 1st 2nd 2nd
C.M.Wells    15    1   56    0                      1st   110    2   43    0
Babington     8    1   28    0     8    1   18    4  2nd   112    2   44    9
Reeve        17    0   58    0     5    1   12    1  3rd   112    2  152   17
Mays         31   10   78    3     6    0   17    0  4th   112   30  267   17
Standing     16    6   26    0                       5th   152   50  273   17
                                                     6th   265   60  290   31
GLOUCESTERSHIRE                                      7th         67  315   57
Lawrence     11    1   34    4    10    0   57    0  8th         84  328   62
Walsh        17    5   34    2    28.1  5   95    4  9th        101  333   82
Bainbridge    5    1   12    0     2    0    7    0 10th        102  341
Graveney     11.4  4   17    4    25    7   61    1
Lloyds        1    1    0    0    30    2  111    5

Umpires: M.J.Kitchen and R.A.White
```

Twelve runs were still needed as a hobbling 'Syd' Lawrence made his way out to join Jack Russell, but the injured pace bowler then hooked Imran for a mighty six. He also bravely scrambled some singles to see Gloucestershire home by one wicket, typifying both the character among the new breed of West Country players and the spirit that under Alleyne's astute leadership has carried Gloucestershire to their successes in recent years.

DERBYSHIRE

25, 27, 28 July 1987 at Bristol

Nothing ventured, nothing gained – that was the refreshing attitude of Derbyshire's young captain Kim Barnett (seen below), and in these days of three-day county matches it often needed such a positive outlook and shrewd negotiations with fellow captain for the contests to reach a positive outcome. This is precisely what happened when Barnett's team played at Bristol in 1987, and after a generous declaration by the visiting captain, the game ended in a dramatic tie.

The previous couple of days had seen four players on each side record half-centuries as the visitors gained a lead of 52. Barnett then hit a century before lunch on the final day against a Gloucestershire attack missing both captain David Graveney and Courtney Walsh, their West Indian spearhead. Without two of their leading bowlers, the Gloucestershire attack was plundered for 167, but this was merely the hors d'oeuvre before Barnett's lunchtime declaration that set Gloucestershire a target of 279 to win in the remaining four hours.

With Michael Holding, the masterful West Indian pace bowler, in the Derbyshire side, some felt that the target might be too much for Gloucestershire, but it was two of the lesser lights in the Peakites attack – off-spinner Reg Sharma and seamer Roger Finney – who proved to be the most effective, as Gloucestershire stuttered to 125 for 5.

Kim Barnett, who played county cricket
for both Derbyshire and Gloucestershire.

```
                        GLOUCESTERSHIRE v DERBYSHIRE

Played at Bristol on 25th, 27th, 28th July 1987          Toss: Derbyshire
Match Tied

                                 DERBYSHIRE
K.J.Barnett *     c Bainbridge b Lawrence   80        lbw       b Bainbridge 110
B.J.M.Maher +     c Russell    b Lawrence    5                  b Lawrence     1
B.Roberts         c Russell    b Walsh      53        c Russell b Lloyds      69
J.E.Morris                     b Walsh       6        c Bainbridge b Lloyds    0
R.J.Finney        c Romaines   b Walsh       0        st Russell b Bainbridge 28
R.Sharma          st Russell   b Lloyds     55
I.S.Anderson      c Russell    b Lawrence   59
M.A.Holding                    b Walsh       9 ( 6)     not        out         2
M.Jean-Jacques                 b Lloyds     15
M.Beardshall      c Russell    b Lawrence   25
O.H.Mortensen          not        out        5
   Extras         (b 7, lb 18, w 1, nb 2)   28        (b 4, lb 8, nb 4)       16
                                           ---                                ---
   TOTAL                                   340        (for 5 wkts dec)       226

                               GLOUCESTERSHIRE
A.W.Stovold       c Morris     b Mortensen  11                  b Finney      51
A.J.Wright        c Barnett    b Holding    14        lbw       b Sharma       2
P.W.Romaines          lbw      b Holding     8        lbw       b Sharma      16
P.Bainbridge      c Barnett    b Sharma     53                  b Sharma      20
K.M.Curran        c Beardshall b Holding     0        c Sharma  b Finney      24
J.W.Lloyds        c Holding    b Finney     66                  b Holding     64
M.W.Alleyne                    b Sharma     51        c Maher   b Finney      53
R.C.Russell +     c Holding    b Finney     54          not       out         19
D.V.Lawrence          lbw      b Sharma      0 (10)             b Sharma      14
C.A.Walsh                      b Finney     14 (11)             b Sharma       0
D.A.Graveney *         not        out        1 ( 9) c Barnett   b Sharma       1
   Extras         (b 6, lb 4, w 1, nb 5)    16        (lb 10, nb 4)           14
                                           ---                                ---
   TOTAL                                    288                              278

GLOUCESTERSHIRE   O    M    R    W     O     M    R    W     FALL OF WICKETS
Walsh             27   6    77   4                              D    G    D    G
Lawrence          14.3 1    61   4    15    1    47   1       1st  27  1st  2nd 2nd
Lloyds            30   4    86   2    22    1    95   2       1st  27   17    7   18
Bainbridge        12   2    34   0    14.1  1    56   2       2nd 134   32  174   71
Graveney          30   7    57   0                           3rd 140   38  174   73
Alleyne                               2     0    16   0       4th 142   42  211  119
                                                             5th 165  132  226  125
DERBYSHIRE                                                    6th 242  198       221
Holding           17   2    74   3    20    1    76   1       7th 255  256       249
Mortensen         8    3    11   1                            8th 290  256       258
Sharma            24   4    63   3    32    12   80   6       9th 331  281       278
Jean-Jacques      4    0    27   0    5     0    29   0      10th 340  288       278
Barnett           8    0    48   0
Beardshall        5    0    16   0
Finney            16   6    39   3    19    1    83   3

Umpires: K.E.Palmer and P.B.Wight
```

Barnett's admirable intentions looked like being rewarded, but Jeremy Lloyds and Mark Alleyne then revived the run chase, adding 96 runs for the sixth wicket before Holding disposed of Lloyds. Jack Russell then joined forces with Alleyne and with Barnett persevering with Sharma's spin at one end, the game reached its dramatic conclusion.

Russell brought the scores level with three balls remaining, and when Lawrence drove Sharma's next delivery, it looked as if he had struck the winning runs. But Barnett made a wonderful diving stop, and both bowler and fielder were rewarded as Sharma then bowled Lawrence, before yorking Walsh with the final ball to leave the game tied with honours even – a fitting end to a fine game of cricket.

SURREY

The pages of cricket's history books are littered with heroic deeds and brave batting performances by tailenders – the game with Surrey at the Cheltenham Festival in 1988 nearly saw the names of all-rounder Kevin Curran and fast-medium bowler Terry Alderman added to these as the Zimbabwean and Australian joined forces to nearly win the game for their adopted English county.

With the West Indies touring Britain, Alderman had been signed as a direct replacement in the bowling department for Courtney Walsh. The Caribbean paceman had few pretensions with the bat, so Alderman's abilities as a combative tail-end batsman were an added bonus, and the Australian put these batting talents to good use in this classic match as Gloucestershire chased 265 on the final day.

Surrey had earlier been dismissed for 115 by the rampant David Lawrence, who more than filled Courtney Walsh's shoes, by taking what was a career-best 7/47 in a display of controlled aggression and hostility that greatly assisted his quest of a place in the England team. For their part, Surrey also had a hostile West Indian pace bowler in their ranks in the form of the fearsome Sylvester Clarke, and he had already demonstrated his abilities by taking five wickets in Gloucestershire's first innings as well as breaking two of Bill Athey's knuckles in his right hand. Bravely he returned to the crease to help Alderman see Gloucestershire past the follow-on, before David Graveney declared.

The damage caused by Clarke was not over as Gloucestershire began their run chase, and the West Indian took the first four wickets as the home team moved on to 82 for 4. With Nick Peters hitting his straps at the other end, this soon became 132/8, and with Athey unable to bat, Surrey were just one wicket away from victory. But up stepped Kevin Curran to match fire with fire, and

The Princess of Wales meets a group of Gloucestershire players – Bill Athey (extreme left), David Lawrence, kevin Currah, phil Bainbridge, tony Wright and (obscured) Courtney Walsh.

```
                           GLOUCESTERSHIRE v SURREY

Played at Cheltenham College on 30th July, 1st, 2nd August 1988 Toss: Gloucestershire
Surrey beat Gloucestershire by 21 runs

                                  SURREY
G.S.Clinton      c Stovold    b Lawrence   102 ( 8)      not          out      18
P.D.Atkins       c Stovold    b Alderman    17 ( 1) c Russell    b Lawrence     0
A.J.Stewart      c Alleyne    b Lawrence    21         c Curran    b Lawrence   0
M.A.Lynch        c Wright     b Curran      45         c Curran    b Alderman   0
D.M.Ward         c Russell    b Curran      43         c Wright    b Lawrence   4
C.J.Richards +   c Russell    b Alderman    43                     b Lawrence  18
I.A.Greig *      c Athey      b Alderman     0         c Stovold   b Alderman   35
K.T.Medlycott    c Wright     b Alderman     1 ( 2) c Russell    b Curran     17
N.H.Peters       c Russell    b Curran       8                     b Lawrence   0
S.T.Clarke                    b Curran      16         c Alleyne   b Lawrence  11
M.P.Bicknell        not         out          8                   c & b Lawrence 5
     Extras      (lb 7, nb 1)                8         (lb 2, w 1, nb 4)        7
                                            ---                                ---
     TOTAL                                  312                                115

                               GLOUCESTERSHIRE
A.W.Stovold      c Stewart    b Bicknell     5         c Stewart   b Clarke    46
A.J.Wright       c Richards   b Clarke       1         c Ward      b Clarke    27
P.Bainbridge     c Medlycott  b Bicknell     3 ( 4) c    sub      b Clarke     0
C.W.J.Athey         not         out         25            absent     hurt
D.A.Graveney *   c Clarke     b Bicknell    13 ( 8) c Richards  b Clarke      5
P.W.Romaines     c Ward       b Clarke      33 ( 3) c Peters    b Clarke      2
K.M.Curran       c Ward       b Clarke      52 ( 5) c    sub     b Clarke    101
M.W.Alleyne                   b Peters      10 ( 6) c Richards  b Peters      8
R.C.Russell +    c Richards   b Clarke       4 ( 7) c Clarke    b Peters      5
D.V.Lawrence     c Bicknell   b Clarke       4 ( 9) c Stewart   b Peters      0
T.M.Alderman        not         out          1 (10)      not         out     43
     Extras      (b 6, lb 5, nb 1)          12         (lb 3, w 1, nb 2)       6
                                            ---                                ---
     TOTAL        (for 9 wkts dec) 163                                        243
```

```
GLOUCESTERSHIRE   O    M    R   W      O     M    R   W     FALL OF WICKETS
Lawrence         21    3   85   2    14.5   0   47   7          S    G    S    G
Alderman         20    1   81   4     8     1   42   2        1st  1st  2nd  2nd
Bainbridge       14    2   40   0                        1st   32    5    0   74
Curran         23.2    6   62   4     6     1   24   1    2nd   55    9    1   75
Graveney         12    1   37   0                        3rd  116    9    4   75
                                                         4th  249   37   17   82
SURREY                                                   5th  264  141   41  103
Clarke         21.1    5   44   5    32.1  14   63   6    6th  265  144   46  109
Bicknell         14    4   49   3    20     2   68   0    7th  267  151   94  125
Peters           13    3   44   1    20     1   96   3    8th  280  155   96  132
Greig             5    1   13   0     6     2   13   0    9th  300  162  108  243
Medlycott         1    0    2   0                        10th  312       115

Umpires: D.J.Constant and B.J.Meyer
```

with valiant support from number eleven Alderman, the College scoreboard kept ticking over; in fact so much so at one stage that Surrey had to deploy all of their fielders around the boundary boards in a bid to stem the torrent of runs from Gloucestershire's final pair.

This was not cricket for the faint-hearted as Clarke furiously ran in and with a volley of bouncers and other wicked deliveries attempted to break the stubborn stand. But Curran and Alderman were equal to this joust, and as Clarke became increasingly frustrated, he was warned for persistent short-pitched bowling.

Curran could be an abrasive opponent, but nobody who saw him that day stand up to Clarke could question his heart, or commitment to the Gloucestershire cause, and bristling with aggression, he reached a memorable century after hitting fifteen crisply timed fours. His stand with Alderman had reached 111, when Curran's heroic defiance was ended by another hostile delivery from Clarke, and Surrey had won a remarkable game by 21 runs.

SUSSEX

The Cheltenham College ground has witnessed many match-winning innings by Gloucestershire batsmen. Bill Athey's masterly 181 against Sussex in 1992 must rate with some of the finest, especially as in their first innings the Gloucestershire batsmen had struggled handling the contrasting spin of Brad Donelan and Ian Salisbury.

In fact, some observers felt that Allan Wells, the visiting captain, had been far too conservative in not declaring the Sussex second innings until his side were 345 runs ahead, and based on what had happened in the home county's first innings, they argued that Donelan and Salisbury would need only half of the 92 overs remaining to bowl Sussex to victory.

Their gloomy predictions looked like coming true as opening batsman Dean Hodgson, who had been the sheet-anchor of Gloucestershire's first innings, retired hurt without scoring, but in the end these projections proved to be wildly inaccurate as Athey played his finest innings in Gloucestershire colours.

Bill Athey

```
                        GLOUCESTERSHIRE v SUSSEX

Played at Cheltenham College on 24th, 25th, 27th July 1992      Toss: Sussex
Gloucestershire beat Sussex by 4 wickets

                              SUSSEX
D.M.Smith                   b Ball       61    c Davies    b Ball      23
J.W.Hall        c Russell   b Walsh       8    c Athey     b Davies    34
N.J.Lenham      c Wright    b Alleyne    83                b Scott     52
A.P.Wells *     st Russell  b Davies     63    c Hodgson   b Davies    20
M.P.Speight            c & b Babington    5    lbw         b Ball       7
P.Moores +      c Russell   b Walsh      48    c Russell   b Ball      29
C.C.Remy                    b Walsh      42    c Walsh     b Ball      16
B.T.P.Donelan        lbw    b Walsh       0    not         out         28
A.C.S.Pigott    c Athey     b Davies      0    c Walsh     b Ball       2
I.D.K.Salisbury c Athey     b Davies      2    lbw         b Davies    24
E.S.H.Giddins        not    out           1
Extras          (b 5, lb 4, nb 2)        11    (b 4, lb 1, w 1, nb 1)   7
                                        ---                           ---
   TOTAL                                 324    (for 9 wkts dec)       242

                        GLOUCESTERSHIRE
G.D.Hodgson     c Wells     b Salisbury  82        retired     hurt      0
C.W.J.Athey     c Salisbury b Giddins    22    c   sub     b Pigott    181
A.J.Wright *    c Smith     b Giddins     0    c Moores    b Giddins    21
M.W.Alleyne                 b Donelan    21    c Moores    b Salisbury  46
R.J.Scott       c Wells     b Donelan     1    c Wells     b Giddins     5
R.C.Russell +   c Moores    b Donelan    41    c   sub     b Giddins    57
J.T.C.Vaughan   c Wells     b Donelan     8 ( 8)    not     out         19
M.C.J.Ball      c Moores    b Donelan     4 ( 9)    not     out          6
C.A.Walsh                   b Salisbury   2 ( 7)            b Pigott      0
M.Davies             not    out           2
A.M.Babington   c Salisbury b Donelan    15
Extras          (b 3, lb 14, w 1, nb 5)  23    (b 1, lb 3, w 4, nb 3)   11
                                        ---                            ---
   TOTAL                                 221    (for 6 wkts)           346
```

GLOUCESTERSHIRE	O	M	R	W	O	M	R	W	FALL OF WICKETS			
										S	G	S	G
Walsh	17.2	6	39	4	6.5	2	19	0			1st	1st	2nd	2nd
Babington	15	0	55	1	1	0	14	0					
Vaughan	6	1	25	0					1st	13	62	56	38
Scott	12	3	38	0	5	0	19	1	2nd	109	66	68	125
Ball	17	1	86	1	25	2	101	5	3rd	202	108	102	134
Davies	16	3	47	3	20.3	1	84	3	4th	209	112	111	314
Alleyne	5	2	25	1					5th	243	174	168	315
									6th	301	197	168	321
SUSSEX									7th	301	201	191	
Pigott	3	1	5	0	13	0	48	2	8th	302	204	201	
Giddins	12	4	35	2	19.1	5	60	3	9th	316	206	242	
Remy	9	2	23	0	3	0	12	0	10th	324	221		
Donelan	36.2	13	77	6	29	4	102	0					
Salisbury	30	9	64	2	27	4	120	1					
Lenham	1	1	0	0									

Umpires: R.Julian and B.J.Meyer

The former Yorkshire opener was soon into his stride, and despite the loss of captain Tony Wright, he kept his side well ahead of the required run rate. During his five-hour exhibition of stroke-play, Athey unfurled some immaculately timed strokes and deftly placed drives, and he shared in a series of assertive partnerships, initially with Mark Alleyne and then later with Jack Russell, who made a well-crafted half-century in a fourth-wicket stand of 180 with Athey.

Their combined efforts guided Gloucestershire closer and closer to their target, and by the time he holed out at long leg against Tony Pigott, Gloucestershire needed just 32 more runs. Justin Vaughan, the New Zealander doctor who had joined the West Country side, then manoeuvred the tail-enders past the target with five balls to spare.

GLAMORGAN

23, 24, 25, 26 August 1995 at Abergavenny

There are few batsmen who can lay claim to have scored over 300 runs in a match and establish a major world record, yet still watch almost in horror as his team's last pair fought to save the match in the closing overs. But this is what happened to Andrew Symonds during Gloucestershire's visit to Glamorgan's delightful ground at Abergavenny in 1995.

It had already been an eventful first summer in county cricket for the twenty-year-old Anglo-Australian, with both the land of his birth and the land of his education vying for his services in Test cricket. The Birmingham-born batsman had already established his credentials with centuries against Surrey, Somerset and Essex, and in this next classic match at Abergavenny, Symonds became Gloucestershire's youngest ever double centurion in Championship cricket, in addition to creating a new world record with an explosive display of six-hitting.

There had been no suggestion of anything out of the ordinary as Glamorgan opted to bat first, and if anything, it looked as if the bowlers might prosper as Glamorgan collapsed from 145 for 1 to 203 for 8, before some tail-end defiance from Darren Thomas, Neil Kendrick and Steve Watkin steered the Welsh county to 334.

Then it was the turn of the Gloucestershire batsmen to struggle, as Watkin and West Indian seam bowler Hamish Anthony reduced the visitors to 79 for 4. This was the cue for Symonds to walk to

Andrew Symonds

Steve Watkin, the
Glamorgan bowler
who eventually
dismissed Symonds.

the wicket, but no sooner had he taken guard than his captain Mark Alleyne departed without
addition to the score.

Symonds then took the game by the scruff of the neck, and in the course of the next few hours,
Symonds shared a remarkable partnership of 213 with Reggie Williams, the county's reserve
wicketkeeper. During this time Symonds struck a record salvo of 16 sixes, breaking the previous world
best of 15 struck by John Reid for Wellington against Northern Districts in 1962/63. Admittedly, the
delightful ground did not have the longest boundaries on the county circuit, but most of Symonds
sledgehammer blows were struck with such brutal power and height that they would have sailed for
six on most Test match grounds. Symonds added 22 fours to his tally of 16 sixes and when the final
Gloucestershire wicket fell he was unbeaten on a career-best 254 with his side 127 runs ahead.

GLAMORGAN

With the wicket remaining docile, it was then the turn of the Glamorgan batsmen to prosper as David Hemp and Matthew Maynard each scored hundreds and shared a vibrant third-wicket partnership of 302 as Glamorgan ended the third day on 420-2. The pair only added a further four runs on the final morning as Javagal Srinath proved that wicket-taking was perfectly possible on the shirt-front wicket. With a deft change of pace the Indian seamer took career-best figures of 9/76 to completely rein back Glamorgan's hopes of compiling a target that might be immune from Symonds' bludgeoning blows.

Srinath's efforts meant that Gloucestershire required 345 in the remaining 77 overs, and after his first innings display a few Welsh wags were speculating on how long it would take Symonds and his colleagues to reach this target. But Darren Thomas briefly raised native hopes reducing the visitors to 83 for 3, before Symonds arrived at the crease. There was talk of 'I told you so' as the young tyro continued his six-hitting spree, adding a further four to go past the previous world record of 17 set by Warwickshire's Jim Stewart in 1959.

But with his score on 76, he was trapped leg before by Watkin and with rain clouds gathering and adding to the equation, Watkin and Thomas turned the game around with a brace of wickets. Rather than romping towards their target, Gloucestershire were now left fighting to save the game. The experienced Monty Lynch oversaw their rearguard action, but when Watkin removed Kamran Sheeraz, there were still twenty balls remaining for Lynch and last man Viv Pike to survive.

As Darren Thomas steamed in for the final over, it looked as if there might be a dramatic ending, as firstly a loud appeal was turned down, and then off the last ball, a thick edge from Pike lobbed just over the head of Glamorgan's short-leg fielder. The crowd drew breath but the ball fell safely to earth and Gloucestershire's last pair had survived in one of the most eventful drawn games in their history.

GLAMORGAN v GLOUCESTERSHIRE

Played at Abergavenny on 23rd, 24th, 25th, 26th August 1995   Toss: Glamorgan
Match Drawn

GLAMORGAN

A.J.Dalton		lbw	b Srinath	0		lbw	b Srinath	12
H.Morris *		lbw	b Ball	67	c Windows		b Srinath	62
D.L.Hemp	c Symonds		b Ball	71		lbw	b Sheeraz	157
M.P.Maynard		lbw	b Ball	10			b Srinath	164
P.A.Cottey			b Srinath	7	c Williams		b Srinath	10
A.D.Shaw +			b Srinath	0	c Wright		b Srinath	2
R.D.B.Croft	c Williams		b Srinath	2	c Alleyne		b Srinath	8
H.A.G.Anthony	c Wright		b Ball	4			b Srinath	0
S.D.Thomas		not	out	78	c Williams		b Srinath	3
N.M.Kendrick			b Sheeraz	21	c Hancock		b Srinath	10
S.L.Watkin			b Pike	24		not	out	6
Extras	(lb 13, w 7, nb 30)			50	(b 13, lb 13, w 5, nb 6)			37
				---				---
TOTAL				334				471

GLOUCESTERSHIRE

A.J.Wright	c Hemp		b Watkin	31	c Anthony		b Thomas	23
M.G.N.Windows		lbw	b Watkin	0			b Thomas	24
T.H.C.Hancock			b Anthony	12	c Shaw		b Croft	14
M.A.Lynch		lbw	b Anthony	32 (7)		not	out	56
M.W.Alleyne *			b Thomas	2 (4)	c Dalton		b Thomas	64
A.Symonds		not	out	254 (5)		lbw	b Watkin	76
R.C.J.Williams +	c Kendrick		b Croft	52 (6)	c Shaw		b Thomas	17
M.C.J.Ball		lbw	b Kendrick	2		c sub	b Thomas	2
J.Srinath	c Morris		b Croft	39			c & b Watkin	1
K.P.Sheeraz			b Watkin	3	c Maynard		b Watkin	0
V.J.Pike	c sub		b Croft	22		not	out	0
Extras	(lb 2, nb 10)			12	(b 3, lb 5, nb 8)			16
				---				---
TOTAL				461	(for 9 wkts)			293

GLOUCESTERSHIRE	O	M	R	W	O	M	R	W
Srinath	20	6	74	4	21	3	76	9
Sheeraz	23	3	103	1	14	3	72	1
Alleyne	17	5	59	0	12	3	59	0
Ball	33	9	54	4	26	8	74	0
Pike	9.3	1	31	1	31	6	97	0
Symonds					15	1	52	0
Hancock					2	0	15	0
GLAMORGAN								
Watkin	24	3	122	3	16	3	51	3
Anthony	18	3	81	2	10	1	45	0
Thomas	18	3	100	1	17	0	99	5
Croft	26.5	6	90	3	19	5	70	1
Kendrick	10	0	66	1	4	0	20	0

FALL OF WICKETS

	Gm	Gs	Gm	Gs
	1st	1st	2nd	2nd
1st	0	11	41	43
2nd	145	36	118	58
3rd	166	72	424	83
4th	189	79	440	204
5th	189	79	440	229
6th	191	292	448	236
7th	198	295	448	249
8th	203	379	455	263
9th	276	394	458	277
10th	334	461	471	

Umpires: J.W.Holder and P.B.Wight

NORTHAMPTONSHIRE

29, 30, 31 August, 2 September 1996 at Bristol

I doubt if there has ever been a more aptly named cricketer than Jack Russell to play a leading role in a real dogfight of a match. The contest in question was Gloucestershire's match with Northamptonshire at the end of August 1996.

Tenacity has always been a hallmark of Russell's batting, and in both innings of this classic match, he gave ample demonstration that those in higher circles who had surprisingly dismissed his abilities as a batsman earlier in his career had been very rash indeed. Instead, the man who was regarded by many as the best wicketkeeper in the world produced two pugnacious cameos.

After a first-innings half-century, Russell shared in a seventh wicket stand of 115 with Richard Davis, the former Kent spinner, and the Gloucestershire wicketkeeper confounded the youthful Northants team by mixing the orthodox with the bizarre. Whichever mode he chose, the left-handed Russell was equally effective, and in each innings he ended up as Gloucestershire's top scorer.

His determined efforts meant that the visitors required 243 to win. They had more than a day and a half at their disposal, but it looked as if the game would finish on the third day as Northants slipped to 66 for 5 with David Capel the only top-order batsman remaining at the wicket. But the former England all-rounder then received useful support from his wicketkeeper David Ripley, who after Russell's display, seemed intent on showing his own capabilities with the bat.

Courtney Walsh eventually sent both men back to the pavilion, but not before they had further reduced the target, and with Jeremy Snape and Kevin Innes maintaining the impetus, the spirited run chase continued. Walsh, drawing on his vast experience at Test and county level, shrewdly

Jack Russell

```
                    GLOUCESTERSHIRE v NORTHAMPTONSHIRE

Played at Bristol on 29th, 30th, 31st August, 2nd Sept 1996    Toss: Gloucestershire
Gloucestershire beat Northamptonshire by 15 runs
                              GLOUCESTERSHIRE
D.R.Hewson        c Innes    b Ambrose      0            lbw      b Taylor      3
M.G.N.Windows     c Ripley   b Ambrose      6     c Ripley       b Capel       4
A.Symonds           lbw      b Penberthy   38     c Innes        b Taylor     21
R.I.Dawson          lbw      b Capel       21     c Ripley       b Capel      20
M.A.Lynch         c Ripley   b Capel        6            lbw      b Ambrose    9
M.W.Alleyne       c Ambrose  b Penberthy    0            lbw      b Innes     23
R.C.Russell +     c Ambrose  b Capel       50     c Montgomerie  b Snape      75
R.P.Davis         c Sales    b Curran       7            c & b Penberthy      43
M.C.J.Ball                   b Penberthy    7 (10)         b Ambrose          4
A.M.Smith         c Ripley   b Taylor      15 (11)        not      out        19
C.A.Walsh *         not        out         10 ( 9)         lbw      b Snape    12
    Extras        (b 1, lb 7, w 1, nb 14)  23     (b 4, lb 8, nb 4)           16
                                          ---                                 ---
    TOTAL                                 183                                 249

                             NORTHAMPTONSHIRE
R.R.Montgomerie     lbw      b Alleyne     20            b Smith               5
A.J.Swann           lbw      b Smith        2            lbw      b Alleyne   14
D.J.Capel         c Ball     b Alleyne     18     c Russell      b Walsh      39
D.J.G.Sales       c Lynch    b Alleyne     10     c Russell      b Alleyne     2
K.M.Curran *      c Russell  b Walsh       52     c Hewson       b Symonds    13
A.L.Penberthy     c Davis    b Smith       19            lbw      b Symonds    2
K.J.Innes           lbw      b Smith        3 ( 8)         b Alleyne         20
D.Ripley +          not        out         20 ( 7) c Lynch       b Walsh      36
J.N.Snape           lbw      b Smith        9            lbw      b Smith     33
C.E.L.Ambrose       lbw      b Smith       11     c Lynch        b Walsh      11
J.P.Taylor                   b Walsh        6            not      out         13
    Extras        (b 4, lb 4, nb 12)       20     (b 12, lb 9, w 2, nb 16)    39
                                          ---                                 ---
    TOTAL                                 190                                 227
```

NORTHAMPTONSHIRE	O	M	R	W		O	M	R	W		FALL OF WICKETS			
												G	N	G	N
Ambrose	16	4	34	2		22.2	9	35	2			1st	1st	2nd	2nd
Taylor	18.5	9	38	1		21	5	61	2		1st	0	6	3	7
Capel	13	2	34	3		13	1	37	2		2nd	19	39	27	47
Penberthy	16	1	50	3		17	5	43	1		3rd	69	48	31	49
Curran	6	2	19	1		6	2	21	0		4th	75	81	48	62
Innes						5	0	17	1		5th	78	125	62	66
Snape						14	5	23	2		6th	86	130	95	108
											7th	131	143	210	151
GLOUCESTERSHIRE											8th	152	157	212	179
Walsh	21	8	44	2		28	9	62	3		9th	158	173	226	201
Smith	24	11	68	5		18.4	6	40	2		10th	183	190	249	227
Alleyne	16	4	69	3		23	9	49	3						
Ball	1	0	1	0		11	3	34	0						
Symonds						10	4	21	2						

Umpires: B.Leadbeater and R.A.White

rotated his bowlers, and his inventiveness was rewarded with further wickets as the visitors slumped to 201/9 shortly before the close.

Sensing that victory was near, Gloucestershire claimed the extra half hour, but Snape and Paul Taylor stoutly defended and with a combination of good skill, plus the odd slice of luck, they added a further 17 runs before the close. The Northants resistance continued the following morning as the visitors hastily scampered a few singles, but after several abortive appeals, left-armer Mike Smith ended the contest in Gloucestershire's favour by trapping Snape leg before.

Had it not been for Russell's stroke-play earlier in the game, the contest would never have gone into the final day, and as events transpired, Russell's brave batting was the only difference between the two well-matched sides.

DERBYSHIRE

There cannot have been many occasions when any county, never mind Gloucestershire, have claimed seven out of eight bonus points on the first day of a Championship match. But that is what happened against Derbyshire at the 1997 Cheltenham Festival, thanks to two virtuoso performances, firstly from left-arm seamer Mike Smith (below) and then all-rounder Shaun Young, whose audacious batting put the Australian alongside the likes of Grace and Hammond in the county's annals.

This classic match began with Mike Smith proving exactly why he was regarded as the best left-arm swing bowler in English cricket. 1997 was his finest season in Championship cricket, with a haul of 83 wickets, and in the minds of Gloucestershire supporters it was inexplicable why the England selectors should overlook Smith's claims for a Test place. His late in-swing and bounce saw Derbyshire subside inside 28 overs, with Smith taking 6/47.

Then it was the turn of another player unable to claim a place in his national side to take centre stage, as Shaun Young raced to a maiden Championship hundred. The Australian feasted on some

lacklustre bowling as a pulsating first day of the historic festival ended with Gloucestershire on 306 for 4 with Young unbeaten on 156.

The run feast continued the next morning and the rollicking fifth-wicket stand between Mark Alleyne and Young added 244. Alleyne eventually fell three runs short of a cultured hundred, while Young had reached 237 when he was adjudged leg before to Philip DeFreitas. In all, Young had struck 39 fours and 2 sixes in his 350-minute stay at the wicket which saw the Australian record the highest first-class score at Cheltenham since W.G.'s 318* in 1876, and equal Wally Hammond's record for the county's best against Derbyshire.

Needing 364 to avoid an innings defeat, Derbyshire made a better fist of things in their second innings, but with so many runs in the bank, Alleyne was able to maintain attacking fields. Kim Barnett and Matt Vandrau, who had recovered after

```
                          GLOUCESTERSHIRE v DERBYSHIRE

Played at Cheltenham College on 16th, 17th, 18th July 1997        Toss: Derbyshire
Gloucestershire beat Derbyshire by an innings and 35 runs

                                  DERBYSHIRE
A.S.Rollins          lbw       b Smith       6    c Lynch      b Alleyne     44
M.R.May         c Russell      b Smith       5        lbw     b Smith        46
C.J.Adams                      b Smith       0    c Russell   b Alleyne       0
K.J.Barnett     c Russell      b Lewis      58    c Russell   b Young        94
M.J.Vandrau        retired       hurt        1    c Lynch     b Young        54
V.P.Clarke      c Young        b Smith       9    c Lewis     b Young         0
K.M.Krikken +   c Ball         b Young       0    c Ball      b Lewis        37
P.A.J.DeFreitas * c Russell    b Smith       9    c Russell   b Smith        45
A.J.Harris                     b Smith       0    c Wright    b Smith         2
K.J.Dean        c Wright       b Lewis      16       not        out          2
D.E.Malcolm        not           out         1                b Smith        0
      Extras     (lb 7, w 2, nb 6)          15    (lb 3, nb 2)                5
                                            ---                             ---
      TOTAL                                 120                             329

                              GLOUCESTERSHIRE
A.J.Wright      c Adams        b Malcolm     2
N.J.Trainor     c Krikken      b Malcolm     0
T.H.C.Hancock   c Rollins      b DeFreitas  54
M.A.Lynch       c Dean         b Malcolm     8
S.Young            lbw         b DeFreitas 237
M.W.Alleyne *   c Adams        b DeFreitas  97
R.C.Russell +   c Krikken      b Harris     24
R.I.Dawson      c Krikken      b Harris      0
M.C.J.Ball      c Krikken      b Harris     30
A.M.Smith                      b Malcolm     1
J.Lewis            not           out         0
      Extras     (b 1, lb 8, nb 22)         31
                                            ---
      TOTAL                                 484

GLOUCESTERSHIRE   O    M    R    W      O     M    R    W       FALL OF WICKETS
Smith            12    1   47    6    21.4    5   59    4            D    G    D
Lewis             7    0   36    2     20     4   57    1          1st  1st  2nd
Young             7    1   19    1     12     4   25    3     1st   10    1   71
Alleyne           2    0   11    0     18     4   70    2     2nd   10    2   73
Ball                                   29     5   80    0     3rd   21   16  119
Trainor                                 5     1   27    0     4th   41  155  240
Hancock                                 1     0    8    0     5th   45  399  240
                                                             6th   74  434  251
DERBYSHIRE                                                    7th   74  439  325
Malcolm        28.3    2  102    4                            8th  119  483  325
Dean             17    1   73    0                            9th  120  484  329
DeFreitas        28    5   99    3                            10th      484  329
Harris           24    4  124    3
Vandrau           7    1   17    0
Clarke           10    1   60    0

Umpires: D.R.Shepherd and J.F.Steele
```

being hit on the jaw on the opening day, both passed fifty and offered stout resistance before Barnett edged Young to Russell just 6 runs short of a well-deserved century. Barnett had earlier shown great skill against Smith's in-swing, but the left-armer had the last laugh, as he ended with match figures of 10/106.

A call-up to the England team for the Fourth Test soon followed for Smith, but he enjoyed a fruitless time against the Australians at Headingley, although it might have been very different had Graham Thorpe held onto an edge from Matthew Elliott in Smith's third over. But the margins between success and failure in professional sport can be gossamer-thin, and Smith remained wicketless on this, his one and only Test match appearance.

ESSEX

19, 20, 21 August 1998 at Colchester

Success in professional sport is often about the sum of the parts being more important than the individuals themselves, allied to a communal belief in the team's ability. Gloucestershire's collective success in one-day games during the past six years is evidence of this. Their success has also created a positive culture which, allied to Mark Alleyne's shrewd captaincy and management, plus the coaching of John Bracewell, has helped to nurture the emergence of a new generation of 'Glorious Glosters'.

This final classic match epitomised the philosophy that developed during Bracewell's first year as the county's coach, with the assured and confident Gloucestershire side completely overwhelming a downbeat Essex side, and in the process recording the largest ever winning margin in the club's history.

While Courtney Walsh topped and tailed Essex's modest second innings, the architects of this fine victory were Gloucestershire's home-grown talent – batsmen Tim Hancock and Matt Windows, plus seam bowler Jon Lewis and spinner Martyn Ball. On a featherbed of a wicket, Hancock, the twenty-six-year-old right-handed batsman and twenty-five-year-old Matt Windows, the son of former Gloucestershire all-rounder Tony Windows, recorded fine hundreds against the lacklustre Essex attack, none of whom could contain Hancock's strong drives off his legs or Windows wristy cuts and forcing shots off the back foot. In addition, neither were afraid to use their feet against the Essex spinners who found little assistance from the Colchester wicket.

Gloucestershire's total of 564 then assumed even greater proportions as Essex meekly subsided, as twenty-three-year-old Jon Lewis showed his credentials as a seam bowler as Essex slipped

Martyn Ball (right) celebrates another Gloucestershire victory.

```
                        ESSEX v GLOUCESTERSHIRE

Played at Colchester on 19th, 20th, 21st August 1998        Toss: Gloucestershire
Gloucestershire beat Essex by an innings and 281 runs

                              GLOUCESTERSHIRE
R.J.Cunliffe      c Hyam         b Grove        7
T.H.C.Hancock              c & b Law          135
D.R.Hewson        c Hyam         b Grove       44
M.W.Alleyne *     c Peters       b Law         47
M.G.N.Windows     c Law          b Grayson    151
R.I.Dawson                       b Ilott       46
R.C.Russell +     c Ilott        b Law         28
M.C.J.Ball        c Hodgson      b Grayson     32
J.Lewis           c Flanagan     b Such         4
A.M.Smith             not          out          6
C.A.Walsh         c Robinson     b Such         7
     Extras       (b 15, lb 18, w 2, nb 22)    57
                                              ---
     TOTAL                                     564

                                  ESSEX
D.D.J.Robinson    c Alleyne    b Lewis    16        lbw      b Walsh      40
I.N.Flanagan      c Ball       b Hancock  29   c Dawson      b Walsh       6
T.P.Hodgson       c Russell    b Lewis     5   c Russell     b Hancock     4
R.C.Irani         c Ball       b Lewis    36        c & b Hancock          1
A.P.Grayson *                  b Hancock   0                b Ball        28
S.D.Peters        c Walsh      b Hancock   1                b Ball         3
D.R.Law           c Alleyne    b Ball      3   c Cunliffe    b Ball        0
B.J.Hyam +        c Alleyne    b Ball     33   c Windows     b Walsh       3
M.C.Ilott             not        out      35   c Walsh       b Ball        3
J.O.Grove             lbw      b Dawson    3   c Windows     b Walsh       1
P.M.Such                       b Dawson    8        not        out         0
     Extras       (lb 3, w 2, nb 2)        7   (b 5, lb 1, nb 12)         18
                                         ---                             ---
     TOTAL                                176                            107
```

ESSEX	O	M	R	W	O	M	R	W		FALL OF WICKETS		
										G	E	E
Ilott	22	1	81	1						1st	1st	2nd
Grove	27	4	119	2					1st	21	21	19
Irani	16	5	39	0					2nd	144	37	28
Law	17	0	77	3					3rd	253	61	34
Such	48.4	7	168	2					4th	258	61	79
Grayson	15	4	47	2					5th	382	67	85
									6th	448	70	85
GLOUCESTERSHIRE									7th	536	106	92
Walsh	11	2	40	0	12	4	18	4	8th	546	157	101
Smith	9	2	14	0	7	5	9	0	9th	552	166	107
Lewis	11	1	51	3	5	0	17	0	10th	564	176	107
Ball	13	4	29	2	11.1	4	26	4				
Hancock	3	1	5	3	9	4	24	2				
Dawson	5.4	0	34	2	2	0	7	0				

```
Umpires: A.Clarkson and M.J.Kitchen
```

to 61 for 4, with Lewis surprising the home batsmen with movement through the air and bounce from what had hitherto been a placid surface.

'Herbie' Hancock then played a crucial role again, this time with his medium-pace bowling, claiming three wickets in a three-over spell, as Essex were forced to follow-on. Walsh, who had gone wicketless in the first innings, came on as first change and removed opener Ian Flanagan, before Hancock's medium pace accounted for Tim Hodgson and Ronnie Irani. Martyn Ball's clever off-spin then stifled and teased the Essex middle-order, before Walsh returned to finish off the modest Essex resistance.

Gloucestershire were able to head for home shortly after lunch on the third day after recording their biggest ever innings victory, surpassing their win by an innings and 268 runs over Somerset in 1885. It also marked the dawn of a new era in Gloucestershire history and the start of a marvellous period with a series of classic matches in the one-day format of the game.

Other local interest titles published by Tempus

Gloucestershire CCC Greats

ANDREW HIGNELL

Gloucestershire CCC are steeped in tradition, with the history of the West Country club being richly decorated with some of English cricket's most famous names. Indeed, none could be larger than Dr W.G. Grace. This book proudly recalls the generations of illustrious players who have represented Gloucestershire and built on the record-breaking achievements of the immortal Doctor.

0 7524 2416 5

Pilkington to Powergen Gloucester Rugby Club 1990 - 2003

IAN RANDALL

Gloucester is one of rugby's most famous clubs. Home of 'The Shed', Gloucester ended a long period of underachievement by winning the Powergen Cup in 2003, having reached their first domestic cup final for thirteen years. This is the story of the time between the defeat by Bath and the win over Northampton – one of the most dramatic periods in Cherry-and-Whites' history – told through the reminiscences of those directly involved.

0 7524 3120 X

Cheltenham Town FC

PETER MATTHEWS

This collection of images forms a superb pictorial record of the history of Cheltenham Town Football Club since 1970. During this time, of course, the club embarked upon a meteoric rise through the non-League structure that took them from the Southern League to the Second Division. This volume brings the story up to date with a fresh look at the success of the Cotterill era, as well as the Second Division season of 2002/03.

0 7524 3154 4

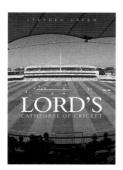

Lord's Cathedral of Cricket

STEPHEN GREEN

The history of the greatest and most evocative sports ground in the world. Lord's: The Cathedral of Cricket, charts the history of the ground from its foundation by Thomas Lord in 1787 through to the twenty-first century stadium with its state-of-the-art media centre. Exciting matches and great events are brought to life in this remarkable book by former museum curator and MCC librarian, Stephen Green.

0 7524 2167 0

If you are interested in purchasing other books published by Tempus, or in case you have difficulty finding any Tempus books in your local bookshop, you can also place orders directly through our website

www.tempus-publishing.com